Clear, Calm, and Connected

CLEAR, CALM, AND CONNECTED

Reflections on Church Leadership

PAUL E. WALTERS AND ROBERT F. HOLLEY

Fortress Press

Minneapolis

CLEAR, CALM, AND CONNECTED

Reflections on Church Leadership

Cover image: bluebeat76 / iStock

Cover design: Emily Harris Designs

Print ISBN: 978-1-5064-6475-6

eBook ISBN: 978-1-5064-6476-3

In thanksgiving for our families: Brandy, Nicholas, Nathan, and Joshua; Janet, Michelle, Rick, Allison, Trey, and Miriam. They have taught us every day about family systems.

CONTENTS

PREFACE

In the hopes of helping you become a better leader, we have written this book to share concepts of family systems theory. This is not a new gospel. It will not replace Jesus, nor will it instantly fix every challenge of your church. What it can do is provide a fresh lens through which to see your congregation or organization. It can help you understand in new ways your own behavior, presence, and functioning.

The prologue touches on core concepts in family systems theory. This section will give you a good sense of what is to follow. But following that, *Clear, Calm, and Connected* does not have to be read cover to cover, like a novel. Instead, each chapter stands alone, with its own questions for discussion or reflection at the end. The chapters can be read in any order, and we hope you will find them an excellent way to begin leadership team meetings, committee meetings, or board meetings.

We have written this book to invite discussion and conversation in times of low anxiety. Our goal is for you and your congregation to work through challenging issues then so when real challenges come and anxiety is higher, you have already practiced such conversations and can respond rather than react.

May this work be a blessing to you and your community. May it lead you to respond and not react, maintain healthy relationships, and proclaim the good news of Jesus faithfully.

Paul E. Walters
Robert F. Holley

PROLOGUE

Has this problem been brewing for months? Pastor Miranda wondered as she sipped her tea and reflected on the conversation she and Alma just had an hour ago. It had ended well, but it could just as well have been a mess, she thought, replaying the meeting in her mind.

Alma was the most talented organist, pianist, and music director with whom Pastor Miranda had worked in her twenty-one years of ministry. An excellent musician, Alma elicited an enthusiastic and harmonious sound from her small volunteer choir. She might have an extraordinarily messy office, but she always planned ahead and gave the secretary hymn selections and special music for the bulletin well in advance. Alma even put together special worship orders for seasonal celebrations such as Good Friday and Christmas Eve—all for a financial pittance.

But today, a conflict that had been stewing for months between the two leaders finally reached a boiling point. Now there was clearly need for clarification. In the past, Pastor Miranda often discussed with Alma the hymns sung at worship. The pastor wanted the first and final hymns to be particularly singable and familiar, to help the congregation start worship well and end with a positive feeling. The other hymns could be new, unfamiliar, and more difficult to sing. Unfortunately, Alma had consistently ignored the pastor's request.

Pastor Miranda had decided Monday was the day to confront the issue head on. She told Alma she was frustrated to find her request ignored week after week. On consecutive Sundays, worship had ended with new and challenging hymns. From Pastor Miranda's vantage point, it looked as if people had stopped trying to sing altogether. Their conversation ended abruptly, interrupted by a phone call for the pastor about a member's medical emergency.

Now it was Thursday afternoon, and Alma had asked for a special meeting to work out their differences. Pastor Miranda was not surprised; several leaders and choir members had mentioned to her that Alma had been complaining about the pastor's request.

Pastor Miranda is well acquainted with family systems theory. This approach recognizes everything is connected. Imagine a circle of five people who are all holding a rope that connects them. If one person steps into the circle, the rope becomes slack. The group's task is to keep the rope taut, so the other four people immediately shift to keep it such. You have a system. The system is maintained by connection and by folks adjusting to change.

The hymn situation is like the group with the rope. Choir members and individuals in the congregation were beginning to complain to the pastor about the hymn selections. We could say the hymn rope was becoming slack. Some folks adjusted by not singing or by not coming to worship at all. Others wanted only the worship committee to select hymns, and still others wanted only the pastor to do it. Everyone was trying to adjust the system so worship would remain meaningful for them.

Pastor Miranda knew it would be best to speak directly to Alma—it is better to talk *to* folks than *about* them. When people speak directly to one another, the system (in this case, the worshipping congregation) can make healthy and helpful adjustments.

But as they sat down together on Thursday, Alma had shared with Pastor Miranda that she almost brought a choir member, Carlos, to their meeting too. Alma was anxious about meeting with the pastor again and thought a third party might help her cause. Carlos could have explained that many choir members liked the new hymns and wanted to sing more of them at every worship service.

***

In family systems theory, they call this a triangle, Pastor Miranda thought as she took a sip of tea. *It's where two folks bring in a third person to reduce the tension between them.* The only problem this creates is a situation in which one person is on the outside and the other two have already formed a tight bond around their solution to the anxiety. This situation damages relationships.

Triangles can entail much more, she remembered, including interlocking triangles. For example, Gail from the choir had wanted to join with the pastor in confronting Carlos because Gail knew not all choir members wanted new hymns every Sunday. The pastor thought carefully and declined Gail's invitation to create a triangle with Carlos.

Knowing triangles can be unhealthy and complicated,

Pastor Miranda had been pleased Alma did not bring Carlos to their meeting. She told Alma how much better it is for just the two of them to work through the problem together. Pastor Miranda had also been pleased with her own decision to leave Gail out of the conversation. There were no triangles this way.

Earlier in the day, Pastor Miranda considered the concept of *cutoff*. Family systems theory tells us people will often react to anxiety in their relationships by going to the extreme of cutting themselves off from others. This way, they avoid having to deal with the anxiety (or so they think).

As she drank her tea, she remembered that Richard, now also a pastor and a longtime friend from their seminary days, recently had such an experience with his organist. They had been close and worked well together. Then one day, out of the blue, his organist resigned and moved to a church across town. Richard never found out why the organist had cut off, but he knew there had been some tension in the congregation, specifically about finances.

Pastor Miranda was relieved Alma was not cutting off. As tough as it was to put the hymn-selecting problem on the table for discussion, doing so could prevent cutting off. The irony is that cutoff only temporarily makes you feel better. The issues causing your anxiety travel with you, even if you distance yourself from a situation. It's better to acknowledge the anxiety and deal with it.

With these thoughts about triangles and cutoff behind her, Pastor Miranda and Alma talked about selecting hymns. "Do you remember," Alma said, "my father was an organist and choir director? He always told me that in those roles you need to challenge a congregation. You need to bring new hymns and tunes into the mix so the congregation grows. You don't want folks to get in a rut and sing only a few hymns over and over."

Pastor Miranda appreciated the reminder about Alma's father—in family systems theory, *multigenerational transmission* often determines the ways in which people react or respond to anxiety. Much of who we are comes down to us through the generations before us. It was clear Alma brought with her what her father used to say in reply to those who did not like the new or difficult hymns he selected. Now, she was using the same words to explain her approach to hymn-selecting.

***

Pastor Miranda continued drinking her tea and reflecting on how each of them found it necessary to do what family systems theory calls *self-differentiation*: defining oneself clearly, remaining calm, and staying connected to others during an anxious situation. Self-differentiation allows us to work through an issue that is prompting anxiety in the system without becoming reactive. Pastor Miranda remembered when anxiety increases in a system, automatic, instinctive, and defensive reactivity can easily dominate everything. Folks let the automatic, instinctive, and defensive emotional process take over. It's not pretty. Defining ourselves clearly, remaining calm, and continuing to connect to others in the midst of the issue allows for a healthier response rather than reactivity.

Pastor Miranda recalled the news story she had watched on TV the previous evening. A police officer had shot an unarmed man who was sitting in his own car. The officer repeatedly told the man to show his hands.

Instead, the man reached for his wallet, yelling, "I don't have a gun!" The officer saw him reaching down and immediately pulled her gun from its holster. One of the things we lose when we become reactive is our ability to hear. We want to fight, take flight, or freeze, so we cannot clearly hear what the other person is saying. Such was the case with this officer, who soon shot and wounded the man in the car.

When anxiety rises, we need to be clear, calm, and connected. We need to move from the part of our brain that is saying "Fight, take flight, or freeze" and enter the part of our brain that allows us to reflect on what is happening, to listen, and to make good decisions. When the automatic, instinctual, and defensive reaction happens, we not only lose our ability to listen, but we also lose our capacity to learn and imagine alternatives. Things can get ugly.

The process of self-differentiation, thought Pastor Miranda, *is what helps us balance our need to be together and to be separate.* Alma loved being part of the music program at St. James Church. It gave her a place to belong among people with whom she shared common interests. Pastor Miranda thought about how, through the church, Alma shared her love of music and her desire to serve the Lord. So many people in the choir and the congregation at St. James Church shared these core values.

Being well self-differentiated, Miranda thought, gave Alma balance. Alma not only spent a great deal of time with others, but she was able to be separate as well. Pastor Miranda reflected on how many hours a week Alma spent at the organ and piano, both practicing and simply playing for her own delight.

As they had talked about selecting hymns, Pastor

Miranda remembered the need to be clear, calm, and connected. She complimented Alma, saying she agreed with her father about the need to challenge the congregation with new hymns. She tried to convey that she fully understood Alma's concern. She heard her clearly, and she was remaining calm and connected with Alma around this goal of keeping the congregation from falling into a rut of singing only old favorites.

**

Miranda thought further about their conversation and recalled Alma reflecting on the rapid pace of change in the world. As a small child, Miranda's grandmother traveled in a covered wagon from Colorado to Oregon; many years later, she flew on an airplane from Los Angeles to Washington, DC, to visit relatives. She had lived to witness lots of change—and it was still happening, only faster than ever.

Alma had pointed out that our society is just like any other system. Society seems to be reactive right now, in a regressive mode. Alma recognized that, in this context, many members want only the familiar when they come to worship. They want to feel there is something not changing rapidly, like the rest of society. Perhaps, Alma conceded, it was not helpful to have too many new and challenging hymns. She began to see Pastor Miranda's perspective in a different light.

Family systems theory calls this *emotional process in society*. Just as an individual can be taken over by the instinctual, defensive, and automatic reaction to anxiety, so can society. Yes, Pastor Miranda thought, our society is a big system, which can be reactive and regressive, or thoughtful and progressive. Perhaps we do need some new hymns so worship does not become stagnant. She and Alma talked about this for almost an hour.

Pastor Miranda thought back to how they ended their discussion. They decided to meet the first Thursday of each month to discuss how new hymns would be selected and used in that month's services. Alma felt affirmed because Pastor Miranda was willing to sing the new and more challenging hymns at worship. Pastor Miranda was hopeful the process of selecting new and challenging hymns together would not burden the congregation with too many, yet still allow St. James's worship to be vibrant.

Pastor Miranda was almost finished with her cup of tea and her reflection on their meeting. She noted how important it was that neither of them had tried to *project* their anxieties onto someone else. For example, they did not shift their anxiety onto the choir or blame them by saying new hymns would be better received if the choir would only sing them more robustly. Both Miranda and Alma knew from past experience that blaming is useless. It does nothing to make a system healthier. Without blaming, they could focus on the future and how singing could further enhance St. James's worship experience.

Draining her teacup, Pastor Miranda noted it was a good meeting and a good cup of tea. Once again, she appreciated how family systems theory helped both Alma and herself be better leaders for the sake of the mission of St. James Church.

***

As you think about your congregation and your leadership, reflect on the encounter between Pastor

Miranda and Alma. You will find elements of family systems theory in the chapters to come: *self-differentiation, cutoff, triangles, family projection, multigenerational transmission, emotional process in society,* and the *nuclear family emotional system.* Being aware of these concepts will help you be a more effective leader in your church and in all aspects of life.

CHAPTER 1.

CLEAR AS MUD OR PLAIN AS DAY

Clarity

> But you are a chosen race, a royal priesthood, a holy nation, God's own people, that you may proclaim the mighty acts of him who called you out of darkness into his marvelous light. (1 Pet 2:9)

"But, pastor, we've never done it this way," Millie said.

She was complaining to Pastor Melody about using laypeople as assisting ministers in worship. The pastor had been trying to explain that everyone is part of the priesthood of all believers. This is an important insight of the Reformation: all of us serve God. Everyone serves in different ways, and many traditions believe a person does not have to be ordained to assist at worship—it's simply an aspect of their service as a priest in the priesthood of all believers.

This was a new and different idea for Millie, and she just didn't get it. She wondered if leading the whole service was too much work for her pastor. Because worship is the center of life in the church, this raises the stakes. Changes in worship tend to trigger anxiety in congregations. To her credit, Millie had come directly to the pastor to talk about this one. Pastor Melody was trying her best to clarify why this change was important.

Clarity is critical in our congregations. Without it, things appear random, or so-called planning is simply the repetition of what has been done in the past. Worse, when there is no clarity, congregations often end up drifting, directionless.

How do we provide clarity? A well-written mission statement is a good place to begin. A mission statement tells the why: Why are we a congregation? Why do we serve in Christ's name? A mission statement brings clarity to leaders. In some ways, the writing process itself is as important as the statement.

There are three requirements for a well-written mission statement:

1. It needs to be only one sentence. That might seem too short, but think of mission statements running for a paragraph or more. Do people even bother to read them? A succinct mission statement is a must.

2. It needs to be understandable. Every organization has its jargon, and the church is no different. If the mission statement is filled with words such as *Eucharist* and *kairos*, no one in the church—let alone outside it—will comprehend it, and it will be ignored.

3. It needs to be easily memorized and remembered. If the statement is brief and understandable, it will be memorable. If no one remembers the mission statement, they won't use it as a guide for their planning, and it will not be able to offer a common goal and theme in times of conflict and challenge.

For example, the Evangelical Lutheran Church in America's mission statement is: "Together in Jesus Christ we are freed by grace to live faithfully, witness boldly, and serve joyfully." This mission statement is sometimes summarized as, "God's work. Our hands." This tagline is clear, concise, and easily remembered. It fits all three of the above requirements.

Here's one instance of a personal mission statement: "I am Marisol, beloved of Jesus, serving." This statement recognizes who Marisol is—she is not someone else and others are not her. She is the unique person she is. "Beloved of Jesus" recognizes her baptism and the loving grace of the cross that has forgiven her and reconciled her to God and others. Finally, "serving" is what she is about as a disciple of Christ. This mission statement brings clarity to who Marisol is, what she does, and how she makes decisions, fulfilling the three requirements.

To bring clarity to a congregation, a well-written mission statement is necessary. Clarity helps us know who we are in Christ and what we are called to do. A mission statement is key to how we make decisions as leaders, and it guides us as we serve in Christ's name. By design, mission statements tend to be broad and act like an umbrella under which decisions about mission can be made. This allows a mission statement to serve a congregation for many years. The mission statement is a big-picture view of things. "God's work. Our hands" is a big-picture reminder of who we are and the one we serve, but it does not explain how the mission is lived out each year.

A second dimension brings clarity to our congregation: we need a vision as well. A vision statement serves as a guide for living out the congregation's mission. While a mission statement might remain the same for years, a vision statement can be revisited annually to adapt to changes in the congregation and community.

Consider a mission statement such as "God's work. Our hands." Scripture tells of Jesus feeding thousands of people on many occasions. Knowing that, it follows God's people would be called to feed people, like Jesus did. A church with this mission statement might include feeding the hungry in its vision statement. Now we have moved from why (mission statement) to how we will serve (vision statement).

Community Church's vision for the coming year, for example, includes feeding the hungry. Here is its vision statement: "As the people of God serving, we will feed the hungry in our community this year. We will have monthly offerings of canned food for the food bank. We will also participate in the Backpacks for Kids program, which provides food at the end of school each Friday for kids who otherwise would not have food for the weekend."

Mission and vision statements often begin through careful and thoughtful reflection on scripture. Consider this passage and some ways congregations might respond to the account:

> The apostles gathered around Jesus and told him all that they had done and taught. He said to them, "Come away to a deserted place all by yourselves and rest a while." For many were coming and going, and they had no leisure even to eat. And they went away in the boat to a deserted place by themselves. Now many saw them going and recognized them, and they hurried there on foot from all the towns and arrived ahead of them. As he went ashore, he saw a great crowd, and he had compassion for them, because they were like sheep without a shepherd, and he began to teach them many things. When it grew late, his disciples came

to him and said, "This is a deserted place, and the hour is now very late; send them away so that they may go into the surrounding country and villages and buy something for themselves to eat." But he answered them, "You give them something to eat." They said to him, "Are we to go and buy two hundred denarii worth of bread and give it to them to eat?" And he said to them, "How many loaves have you? Go and see." When they had found out, they said, "Five, and two fish." Then he ordered them to get all the people to sit down in groups on the green grass. So they sat down in groups of hundreds and of fifties. Taking the five loaves and the two fish, he looked up to heaven and blessed and broke the loaves, and gave them to his disciples to set before the people, and he divided the two fish among them all. And all ate and were filled, and they took up twelve baskets full of broken pieces and of the fish. Those who had eaten the loaves numbered five thousand men. (Mark 6:30–44)

In this story, the crowd followed Jesus. It was late in the day and people were hungry. Jesus challenged the disciples to feed the people. The disciples saw only scarcity, that there was not enough, but Jesus saw abundance. What do we see? Bringing a clear vision to our congregations helps folks see strengths and potential—in this case, to see abundance rather than scarcity.

The vision at St. Mary Church, for instance, was to move into the community to care for people and for members to do hands-on work with others. Sam knew the local homeless shelter served dinner each evening. He also knew various churches were donating and preparing the dinner. The cleanup was done by the shelter's residents. Sam suggested to St. Mary's leadership that taking a turn at the shelter one evening each week would fulfill the church's vision of caring and doing hands-on work with others in the community.

St. Mary Church embraced the opportunity enthusiastically. It organized teams, made appropriate arrangements with the shelter, and soon the congregation was feeding the residents one evening each week. This made a difference in the shelter residents' lives, but it also affected the church's cooks and servers. One said, "I bring my teenage daughter with me, and she has really taken to caring for others. I do not have to remind her when it is our turn to cook and serve—she reminds *me*. It has been a life-changing ministry for us."

***

Writing a mission statement is not as challenging as it might seem. Start with scripture. If your church follows the lectionary, consider the readings for the nearest Sunday. Then there are scriptures such as the miracle of the feeding of the five thousand (Luke 9:12–17), as well as the other three Gospels. Read the Beatitudes (Matt 5:3–12).

Consider what the words and deeds of Jesus have to say about faith in these days, then reflect on your congregation. Consider its strengths and what is most important to the congregation. See which words or phrases stand out, then write them down on notecards for everyone to look at. Try to make a phrase or sentence out of what is there. A mission statement is future-oriented, reminds everyone of the one at the center of Christian witness, and points to something larger than themselves.

It is best if this process begins with the leadership board, but before it is complete, find ways to include other groups within the congregation. Not everyone has to love the mission statement, but everyone should be able to nod their head and say, "Yes, this is who we aspire to be as followers of Jesus."

- Do you have a mission statement that fulfills the three requirements?
- What is your vision for this year?
- When making decisions, do you reflect on your mission statement? How does it bring clarity to your decisions?

CHAPTER 2.

EVERYTHING IS CONNECTED

Nuclear Family Emotional System

I am the true vine, and my Father is the vinegrower. He removes every branch in me that bears no fruit. Every branch that bears fruit he prunes to make it bear more fruit. You have already been cleansed by the word that I have spoken to you. Abide in me as I abide in you. Just as the branch cannot bear fruit by itself unless it abides in the vine, neither can you unless you abide in me. I am the vine; you are the branches. Those who abide in me and I in them bear much fruit, because apart from me you can do nothing. (John 15:1–5)

Huggins Hell is located in Great Smoky Mountains National Park. It is one of the more famous laurel hells in the park—a place where the mountain laurel grows so thick you cannot walk through it. People have been known to get lost in these hells for days, surviving on berries growing there.

Like those famous laurel hells, congregations are a tangled mess of relationships. Imagine trying to chart the interconnections of people within a congregation. You might start with your own family relationships, which could include as many as three or four generations all worshipping together. Then come your friendships, shared committees, and volunteer groups. Do people sing in the choir together? Do these couples eat together on a regular basis? Soon enough, you have nothing but a mess of connections, hopefully with Jesus at the center of it all.

Jesus describes humanity as branches growing off of him, the true vine. This means we are all connected to Jesus, but also to one another through Jesus in ways both obvious and subtle. Add to this all the ways the people in a congregation are connected to one another, and vines are crisscrossing everywhere. Everyone in the congregation is part of a big, complex system.

**

Ralph looked up and sighed. "Those tasteless wafers again? This is the third Sunday in a row," he mumbled. His wife, Annie, rolled her eyes, ignoring his grumbling and focusing on the pastor's words as she presided over communion.

After worship, Annie said, "Stop complaining about the wafers. Don't you know a water leak destroyed Judy's daughter's kitchen?"

"What does that have to do with having wafers at communion?" Ralph asked.

"Judy always bakes the bread for communion, but she has been so busy taking care of her grandchildren these past few weeks that she hasn't been able to make it, so we've had to have wafers," Annie said.

"Surely someone can buy the bread?" Ralph suggested bitterly.

"Why are you always so grumpy about everything?"

"Hmmpf." Ralph crossed his arms over his chest. He and Annie didn't speak much the rest of the day.

At first blush, it may seem strange to think a water leak at one home would cause marital strife in another, but things are connected in surprising ways. Leaders are key to congregational systems remaining healthy when anxiety inevitably rises. The challenge is to respond to it in a way that builds up the group. Anxiety can arise over serious and significant issues or seemingly small things, such as the kind of bread used at communion.

***

Imagine you are playing a game. It is a simple and easy one: You purchase a toy, a tube about eight inches long. When you hold both ends, the tube flashes with light because you're completing its electrical circuit. The challenge is to see how many ways you can complete the circuit. Can you hold one end and place the other end on a piece of metal, then touch the metal and see the toy light up? How about standing in a circle with other leaders from your congregation? Hold one end of the toy and give the other to another leader. It will not light up until you join your free hands together to make a circuit. Add a few of the other leaders to the group. When you all hold hands, the toy will light up. But if someone drops their hand or breaks the circuit, the light goes out. The rules of this system are simple.

All leaders are part of the congregational system. Each leader influences the system and is important for it to healthily function. How do you participate in your system to keep your congregation healthy?

As leaders, you realize which bread is used at communion (and many other things) is part of your congregational system. Being well defined yourself and functioning in a healthy manner will influence your congregation's health. Your presence and functioning in the system is key. If you are missing or if you are not connected, the light will not burn brightly.

Congregations are systems in which people are connected. Consider a family as they plan events around their child's baptism. The parents ask the pastor if they can use the church fellowship hall for a reception afterwards—no big deal. But two days after agreeing, the pastor realizes that is the same Sunday another group was going to have its only summer lunch-and-learn day in the space. Now the lunch-and-learn group will have to move to the lounge, and the people who use the lounge for kids' church on Sunday mornings will have to move their classes to the nursery so someone else can set up for the lunch-and-learn class. Everything is connected.

One of the challenges of living together in a community is watching as seemingly unrelated people and activities come into contact. When you add into the mix the emotional component of relationships, situations become even messier. When this kind of mess happens, leaders who are present and functioning in healthy ways are able to help the different groups use their spaces efficiently so all of them can function well in the church system, whether it is at the baptism, the lunch-and-learn, or kids' church. Being present in the system allows leaders to recognize these connections and promote healthy relationships.

***

Have you experienced one of those moments when leadership functions so well that ministry happens right in front of your eyes? It happened at Church of Joy thanks to Hilda, the local refugee resettlement representative. It was her job to find sponsors for refugees fleeing war. She was hard at work, lining up congregations to help. One fall Sunday morning, following worship, Hilda came to speak to the members of the Church of Joy. As worship ended and the congregation sat, Joe, the congregation's president, introduced Hilda.

Hilda began by telling the congregation about her work and what it entailed to sponsor a refugee family. After about ten minutes of the nuts and bolts of sponsoring, she ended her introduction and asked for questions. Phillip immediately raised his hand. "How soon will there be an available refugee family if we decide to sponsor one?" he asked.

Hilda was delighted with the question. "We have families arriving often," she said. "In fact, a family is arriving Thursday, comprised of a grandparent, a mom and dad, and a little girl, eight years old. I had lined up another church to sponsor them, but they have dropped out. So now I am in a bit of a panic, hoping I can find another congregation to sponsor them."

Immediately, Frances raised her hand. "I think Church of Joy can sponsor this family starting Thursday," she said. "These people need our help, and it's our mission to reach out to those who are suffering injustices. I cannot think of a greater injustice than war making you leave your extended family, your friends, your home, your job, your country, and so much more. I am in favor of sponsoring this family. They need us."

Jacquelyn stood and agreed with Frances that the church should financially sponsor the family. Mary offered to help the family get their young daughter into school. Kevin, who worked at the hospital, offered to help them figure out medical care. June offered dental care at her office. In between these offers, several other members pledged $100 or more to the cause.

"It seems we have the Holy Spirit at work here today," Joe said. "I will entertain a motion to sponsor this family, beginning Thursday. Is there a motion?" One was immediately made and seconded. The vote was unanimous.

Church of Joy enthusiastically met the family at the airport that Thursday. The family settled into their apartment and worked diligently at new jobs they were offered and at learning to speak and read English, now their third language. Within two years, they had become home-owning and tax-paying supporters of the community. Church of Joy had done an excellent job of sponsoring them.

One key to this conversation's success was that the church's leadership did not become anxious and interrupt the spirit's enthusiastic movement in the congregation toward the sponsorship. Joe could have said something like, "Well, we're behind in our regular giving and aren't meeting the budget, so I don't think we can do this." Rather, thanks to Joe's calm, clear, and connected leadership, the members assessed the situation, reflected on what they might do, and moved ahead confidently. It was a blessed meeting with outstanding leadership.

This is the web of connection in a group of people. In this example, once a family's need for a sponsor was introduced, suddenly a roomful of people was making plans to help a family start a new life in a new country. The people were willing to drop everything because of the inspiration they found in each other. Focused on a concrete goal, any anxiety about the budget diminished. In this case, all the connections worked together to give a needy family a great start at a new life.

- Where have you seen change in one area of your church's life impact a seemingly unrelated area?

- How can understanding the connections between people and groups at church help you serve faithfully as a leader?

CHAPTER 3.

EVERYONE LOVES A QUICK FIX

Self-Differentiation

Now when Jesus came into the district of Caesarea Philippi, he asked his disciples, "Who do people say that the son of man is?" And they said, "Some say John the Baptist, but others Elijah, and still others Jeremiah or one of the prophets." He said to them, "But who do you say that I am?" Simon Peter answered, "You are the Messiah, the son of the living God." And Jesus answered him, "Blessed are you, Simon, son of Jonah! For flesh and blood has not revealed this to you, but my Father in heaven. And I tell you, you are Peter, and on this rock I will build my church, and the gates of Hades will not prevail against it. I will give you the keys of the kingdom of heaven, and whatever you bind on earth will be bound in heaven, and whatever you loose on earth will be loosed in heaven." Then he sternly ordered the disciples not to tell anyone that he was the Messiah.

From that time on, Jesus began to show his disciples that he must go to Jerusalem and undergo great suffering at the hands of the elders and chief priests and scribes, and be killed, and on the third day be raised. And Peter took him aside and began to rebuke him, saying, "God forbid it, Lord! This must never happen to you." But he turned and said to Peter, "Get behind me, Satan! You are a stumbling block to me; for you are setting your mind not on divine things but on human things." (Matt 16:13–23)

Think of an aha moment you had recently. You know, a moment when the light bulb goes on over your head? Aha moments usually do not happen when we go for the quick fix. Pastor Jones learned a simple lesson in the problem of doing a quick fix—literally. Her lesson began shortly after she and her mission congregation moved into their new building. The building was beautiful, and within a month, the congregation already appreciated having a permanent place for mission and ministry.

It was the dead of winter and temperatures were in single digits, even in the daytime, a bit unusual for the area. Still, Sunday morning services had gone well and Sunday school classes were full. All was well. Then everyone dispersed for lunch, including Pastor Jones.

That afternoon, Pastor Jones received a call from Pedro. He was frantic. He had stopped by the church to pick up his choir music for Sunday when he discovered the whole building was flooding. Water was pouring down through the ceiling of the pastor's office. Quickly, people gathered and shut off the water to the building. Everything was drenched, and the water stood several inches deep in places. The volunteer fire department came, pumped out the water, and set up fans to dry things out. Everyone was upset by this devastating setback. The next day, a company specializing in remediating flooded buildings came to start a week of cleanup.

The contractor who had built the church immediately sent over a plumber to fix the leaking pipe. The pipe belonged to an exterior faucet, and although its shutoff valve had been employed, the pipe had still frozen and broke, allowing water to gush into the building. Within an hour, the plumber had replaced the pipe and all was well again—until the next spring, when someone turned on the shutoff valve so they could use the exterior faucet. The pipe had frozen again. It leaked, but was noticed immediately. The plumber returned and replaced the broken pipe a second time. All was well—until the next year. There it was again, the pipe leaking after freezing and breaking during the winter. Pastor Jones had learned to watch carefully when the shutoff valve was turned on in the spring. By the time the plumber arrived to make the third repair, the plumber and the pastor were on a first-name basis.

Standing in the office with the plumber, Pastor Jones asked where the water pipe went. The plumber explained the pipe traveled diagonally across the office, over the door, then across the building.

"What if we move the shutoff valve from the exterior wall to above the office door?" Pastor Jones asked. "Then when we shut off the water to the exterior faucet for the winter, the pipe will be empty for fifteen feet or more. Is this possible?"

The plumber looked at the ceiling, lifted the ceiling tiles, then peered above the door. "Sure," he said. "And that will mean the shutoff will be in a warmer area of the building." So he moved the shutoff valve and the pipe never froze or leaked again.

The first fix—the quick fix—had not been a good one. But folks were upset and anxious when the new building flooded, and they wanted it fixed immediately. "Get it done," they said. It took two more leaks for someone to stop to think about a better solution, a permanent fix.

Each time the plumber had cut out the leaking section of pipe, he had given it to Pastor Jones. She had set the pipes on her desk. One day, Gerardo, a member, asked if he could have them. Pastor Jones agreed. A few weeks later, Gerardo dropped by the office. He had mounted the three pipes on a lovely piece of wood, and he had lacquered them so they looked like art. Pastor Jones kept the plaque of pipes on her wall to remind her it is best to take time to assess a problem thoroughly rather than jump to a quick fix. Gerardo had given her a gift that would remind her to slow down, evaluate the situation, respond thoughtfully, then move ahead feeling confident they had the best solution whenever she felt as if leaders were jumping to a quick fix.

***

Peter wanted a quick fix when he and Jesus and the other disciples were at Caesarea Philippi. First, Jesus asked who folks thought he was. In response, they gave him the laundry list of John the Baptist, Elijah, or even one of the prophets. Then Jesus asked the disciples for their opinion, and Peter responded with his now-famous confession: "You are the Messiah, the son of the living God." Jesus then proclaimed Peter to be the very rock upon which the church would be built.

Peter: the rock! But it didn't last long. When our Lord Jesus revealed it was necessary that he go to Jerusalem, undergo great suffering, and be killed, only to be raised on the third day, Peter objected. Peter wanted the quick fix. He did not want God's way; he wanted his own quick, easy way. When Peter went for the quick fix, our Lord responded, "Get behind me, Satan." Peter was not doing God's will when going for the quick fix.

Another passage in the Bible illustrates well the quick-fix approach and its results. Here is Exodus 32:1–6:

When the people saw that Moses delayed to come down from the mountain, the people gathered around Aaron and said to him, "Come, make gods for us, who shall go before us; as for this Moses, the man who brought us up out of the land of Egypt, we do not know what has become of him." Aaron said to them, "Take off the gold rings that are on the ears of your wives, your sons, and your daughters, and bring them to me." So all the people took off the gold rings from their ears and brought them to Aaron. He took the gold from them, formed it in a mold, and cast an image of a calf; and they said, "These are your gods, O Israel, who brought you up out of the land of Egypt!" When Aaron saw this, he built an altar before it, and Aaron made proclamation and said, "Tomorrow shall be a festival to the Lord." They rose early the next day and offered burnt offerings and brought sacrifices of well-being, and the people sat down to eat and drink, and rose up to revel.

This is the old story of anxiety rising in a group or system. Moses is late getting back. The folks are nervous and become more so each day. So, they beg Aaron, the second in command, to fix things for them. He is more than happy to oblige; after all, it'll resolve their anxiety and stop their grumbling. He takes the gold, forms the calf, and the people worship this idol and become unfaithful. By giving in so fast to their worry, fear, and anxiety, the people are willing to give up anything, even the one true God, for a quick resolution.

Every congregation has probably experienced going for the quick fix only to later discover they would have been better off slowing down and waiting for emotions to settle and anxiety to dissipate. Sometimes this can be overcome easily, but in other instances, giving in to anxiety brings mission and ministry to a sudden halt. The challenge is to find a way to slow down, take a breath, and give things time to process. This can require courageous leaders, who refuse to take on the anxiety and emotionality of the group as they work toward a larger vision of the future.

- Think about the times when a quick fix has not been helpful to your congregation's mission and ministry. What happened? How did it come about?

- What can be done differently the next time anxious folks ask for a quick fix? Is it possible to slow down, assess the situation calmly, respond thoughtfully, and move ahead, confident that a healthy path has been chosen rather than a tenuous quick fix that will likely end badly?

- When have you taken the time to think things through and avoid the trap of the quick fix?

- Think of an instance in which the anxious need of individuals for a quick fix has influenced the decisions of your leaders.

CHAPTER 4.

COULD I BE THE PROBLEM?

Self-Differentiation

> Wash yourselves; make yourselves clean;
> remove the evil of your doings
> from before my eyes;
> cease to do evil,
> learn to do good;
> seek justice,
> rescue the oppressed,
> defend the orphan,
> plead for the widow. (Isa 1:16–17)

Could I be the problem? Phillip kept asking himself. He was thinking back on the many times he had prevented new ministries from happening at Christ the Servant Church. Sure, he had gone along with the plans for a new preschool—but only after he realized the church would get a cut of the proceeds. For Phillip, it was always about money and the survival of Christ the Servant Church.

Being anxious about these things led Phillip to oppose almost any change at Christ the Servant. Once, Alcoholics Anonymous had requested to use a Sunday school room one night each week for two hours. Phillip immediately opposed their request. It would cost the congregation too much money in utilities. What if there were damage to the building? And cleanup—who would do that, and would Christ the Servant have to pay for it? Who would open and close the building? Who would be responsible?

As Phillip thought about these questions, he had felt his throat constrict and his heart rate increase. He had been anxious, so he called three of his good friends on the board and talked them into opposing AA using the building. He had spent an hour and a half on the phone.

When the board later considered the building use request, Phillip loudly opposed it. Even though Pastor Irma spoke about ministry to the community, the board voted to deny the request.

Then there was the youth's request for the congregation to pay half the cost for the group to attend the national youth convention. Phillip was shocked such a request would even be made. At the board meeting, he made sure it would not happen. Giving was down 3 percent compared to the previous year. Highly anxious, Phillip gave an impassioned speech at the meeting. "Christ the Servant is in no position to pay anything toward the youth trip," he declared, even though there was money allocated for youth in their budget. Celeste rebutted by telling a stirring story about how her trip to a national youth convention had been the turning point in her faith journey. Its impact on her still nurtured her faith today.

Even with that reminder of the value of such events in the faith formation of youth, Phillip restated his opposition, and the board acquiesced. Phillip got his way. Most of the youth could not afford the full cost, so the group did not attend the event.

Phillip had also once anxiously opposed a proposal to renovate the kitchen, led by Pastor Irma (whom Phillip had never liked) and the ladies of the church. *Can you imagine*, he had thought, *they want to replace an already working stove!* It may have been thirty-one years old, it may have been impossible to regulate the oven temperature, but it was still useable. He saw to it that their project was immediately stopped too.

These were a few of many occasions on which Phillip had reacted anxiously to change. His leadership style was to oppose everything except the things they had always done, such as worship and Sunday school. Phillip felt he was the last and only barrier to preventing Christ the Servant from doing crazy things that would ultimately lead to it closing its doors.

Lately, though, he had noticed a clear downturn at Christ the Servant. There were fewer members and lower attendance at worship, Sunday school, and everything else. Why, this past month, Gertrude had told him her son and his family were leaving to join another church nearby, one that fed the homeless at the shelter once each week. Gertrude's son thought this is what faith is about: serving others out of a sense of gratitude for being forgiven and loved by God.

That conversation was still in the forefront of Phillip's mind when Pastor Irma announced at the board meeting that a neighboring congregation was having a workshop about seeing leadership through the lens of family systems theory. She encouraged the entire board to join her in attending. Phillip had always thought Christ the Servant was like one big family, so this workshop caught his attention. Also, he thought he'd better go, lest the rest of the board came back from it with strange ideas about spending lots of money.

The workshop was enlightening. The presenter showed

slides and videos, and had the group do exercises. The board members in attendance even wrote a mission statement for Christ the Servant and began working on a vision for ministry for the year.

But when the presenter said, "A leader influences the process by their presence and functioning," Phillip really began to listen closely. This idea spoke to Phillip. "To be a healthier congregation, each leader needs to regulate their anxiety and be deliberately less anxious when anxiety intensifies in the system," the presenter said. Phillip remembered some of the times he'd let his anxiety get the better of him and recognized the result was always to derail Christ the Servant's ministry and mission. Highly anxious, he had become an expert at blocking new initiatives.

The presenter also said a leader needs to be clear about their thinking regarding the issue at hand. This means, she said, getting up into the thinking part of the brain, rather than staying down in the reptilian part, which focuses on survival—the fight, flight, or freeze part, which is instinctual, automatic, and reactive. She pointed out that better decisions are made when the reflective part of the brain is engaged. *Wow*, Phillip thought. *She's talking about me!*

Finally, the presenter said, all through this process of being clearer and less anxious, a leader needs to remain in contact with others. That comment prompted Phillip to realize he had distanced himself from anyone who disagreed with him. *Hmm*, he pondered, *maybe as a leader I need to listen to everyone, even those with whom I disagree.*

After the workshop, Phillip thought again about his question: *Could I be the problem at Christ the Servant?* He certainly had been on numerous occasions. With his new insight into what it means to be a leader who will help the congregation become healthier, Phillip returned to the next few board meetings at Christ the Servant.

Soon, things began to change. Phillip noticed he was listening to everyone, not just the people who agreed with him. He was conscious of how his presence and functioning affected the board. He became aware that he needed to focus on his own responses, not others'. When he calmly focused on himself, he regulated his anxiety, clearly spoke his perspective, and remained connected. With this in mind, board meetings became more positive for him, and much more was being accomplished in ministry and mission at Christ the Servant. Even worship on Sunday morning was more joyous for Phillip. Focusing on his own responses instead of others' allowed him to be a present and well-functioning leader. *This is good*, he thought.

Then came the board meeting at which Marie brought up the need to resurface and fix the parking lot. Marie pointed out it had been more than twenty years since anything had been done to the parking lot, and it was an eyesore to visitors and members, let alone the neighbors. The broken pavement and the numerous potholes were more like craters on the moon, she said. Just last Sunday, she had seen Ann's wheelchair fall into one of the potholes and she could not get out. The ushers had to lift her and the chair out of the crater.

Listening, Phillip felt himself becoming anxious. His throat was constricting and his heart rate was rising. Fixing the parking lot would cost a lot of money. But this time, rather than giving in to his anxiety and becoming reactive, Phillip quietly took a couple deep breaths. *Marie is right*, he thought. *The lot is unattractive, unsafe, and sends a bad message to visitors. It makes it look like we are going out of business, and it's dangerous.* He had heard about Ann's encounter with the pothole and worried she might be seriously hurt.

Rebecca, the board president, asked if everyone would please respond to Marie. She suggested they go around the table and take turns giving their perspectives. As the conversation circled the table, the number of those in favor of resurfacing the parking lot equaled those against it. Then it was Phillip's turn. "I can only speak for myself," he said. "I am in favor of resurfacing the parking lot. This might surprise some of you. In years past, I have opposed just about everything. On this matter, though, I have listened closely to Marie and everyone else. I am not only willing to make a financial pledge to do this, but I am also willing to co-chair the project. I am convinced this needs to be done, for safety and curb appeal, even though it will cost lots of money. Moreover, I think it would be good stewardship to tithe 10 percent of the funds raised for the parking lot to support the shelter for the homeless. I am convinced serving others as well as ourselves is what God calls us to do."

The room was silent for almost a full minute before the discussion resumed. The board voted unanimously to proceed with resurfacing the parking lot and with tithing 10 percent of the funds raised to support the local shelter. Next, when the issue was presented at the congregational meeting, the entire congregation affirmed the project with a 92–2 vote.

Over the next four months, bids were received, a contractor was hired, and the lot was repaired. Phillip looked at it with delight. It was beautiful. But more importantly, Phillip thought about the many people who had worked together to raise the funds and make it possible. There was a wonderful feeling in the air at Christ the Servant Church. Phillip thought, *This is what it means to be a leader—to influence the process by your presence and functioning.*

Once more, Phillip wondered, *Could I be the problem at Christ the Servant?* Now, he answered himself, *Possibly—but hopefully not.*

- As a leader, how are you present and how do you function in anxious times?
- How do you contribute to or lessen the anxiety in your congregation?

CHAPTER 5.

WHAT'S ON YOUR HEART TODAY?

Self-Differentiation

> For by grace you have been saved through faith, and this is not your own doing; it is the gift of God—not the result of works, so that no one may boast. (Eph 2:8–9)

"What's on your heart today?" Emmaline asked Gina as she brought her bagel and coffee to the table. It was the question Emmaline and Gina always asked as they started their conversation on Thursdays when they met at the Plain View coffee shop. They both looked forward to a little time-out in their busy weeks.

"This week," Gina said, "I can't stop thinking about all the division I see in the world. It all started Sunday morning at church." Gina had gone to the late service at First Church, like she did every Sunday. She had taken her bulletin from the greeter and stepped into the sanctuary. Right away, she'd noticed something was different: a couple was sitting in her usual seat. She was a little disappointed but quickly checked herself, thinking, *It's good to have visitors.*

Right behind the visitors, she had spied Walt in his typical seat. Gina liked sitting in front of Walt. He always had a kind word and a smile for her when they shook hands while sharing the peace.

After worship, Walt had caught up to Gina near the sidewalk. "Gina, how are you? I sure missed you this morning."

"What do you mean?" Gina had asked.

"I can't believe those folks took your seat this morning," Walt had said.

"Well, it's always good to see visitors at church," she'd said.

"Maybe, but not all visitors. They were the sort I'd just as soon not see at First Church."

Gina had been surprised. "Why not? Everyone is welcome here. That's what we sing in that hymn, 'All Are Welcome.'"

"We don't need terrorists at this church. Just look at them—they can't possibly be Christian, coming from some desert in the Middle East. They should find their own church with their own people," Walt had said.

Back at the coffee shop, Gina turned to Emmaline. "I couldn't believe it. I was so surprised, I couldn't speak. I mumbled something like, 'We'll have to talk about it sometime.' He said there was nothing to discuss—they were not welcome."

"I don't know what to say," Emmaline said. "I can't believe someone at our church is so openly racist."

"I thought about it all afternoon Sunday," Gina said. "I was angry, sad, confused. Then I remembered a sermon Pastor Valerie had preached on Ephesians 2."

Pastor Valerie had reminded the congregation that God loves everyone unconditionally. She had said there is no way people can do anything to merit God's love and forgiveness. Everyone falls short and God seeks us again and again, forgiving us and loving us regardless. "As we live in the shadow of the cross, we know the love and forgiveness of God is ours," Pastor Valerie had said. "All are loved; there are no exceptions."

Gina resonated with that, for this promise grounded her life. Everything else grew from that center. She told Emmaline, "As I live in the shadow of the cross, I know God is doing for me what I can't do for myself: giving me life and giving it to me abundantly. This is my core belief."

Pastor Valerie's sermon on Ephesians had reinforced Gina's convictions. When she had heard Walt's harsh words, she knew he was wrong. *All are welcome*, she thought.

"I agree," Emmaline said. "Living in the grace of God, all are welcome in our community of First Church. I am so sorry you had that experience. I am also guessing it is not the first time. I remember you told me years ago that you were born in Mexico and your folks brought you here when you were just a baby. The experience with Walt must've hit close to your heart."

"It did, and I just keep hoping people will listen to sermons like the one Pastor Valerie preached and change. But I can't help but wonder what will happen if Walt finds out the truth about me."

Gina and Emmaline wondered how they could take a stand against the racism Gina had experienced. They considered how she might have a word with Walt that he would hear. They strategized how to convince him to welcome everyone to First Church.

That afternoon, Emmaline was working in her garden. As she pulled weeds and plucked dead branches off plants, she continued mulling over her morning conversation with Gina. She recalled the last First Church board meeting, at which Pastor Valerie had some important words for them. The board had been discussing an upcoming youth event elsewhere, and several board members had not been in favor of the youth attending. They thought it was too expensive and not a good value.

Pastor Valerie had talked that day about the difference between core beliefs and an outer circle of beliefs. This outer circle represents the things we do to get along in this world. Things such as listening carefully to others and being considerate of their opinions when they differ from ours constitute the outer circle of who we are. These are the things we do to live in a safe and pleasant world, like when we stop on red and go on green at traffic lights. Then Pastor Valerie talked about core beliefs. She said a core belief for her was God's unconditional love in Jesus, not because we qualify somehow, but simply because God chooses to claim us in this extravagant love.

Pastor Valerie shared her memories of youth events as a teen. For her, that was a place where she encountered these core beliefs. Youth events are a place where young people receive and explore what it means to have faith that Jesus Christ is Lord of all. Core beliefs are formed across the years, and a special youth event can be the place where a young person forms the most important core beliefs of their lives.

Pastor Valerie then took a few minutes to reflect on Galatians 3:28: "There is no longer Jew or Greek, there is no longer slave or free, there is no longer male and female, for all of you are one in Christ Jesus." This passage had been the theme of a youth event she'd attended as a teen. Now, years later, she still often returned to those holy words. The youth event and its theme were life-changing for Pastor Valerie. There, she came to know and trust in God's love in the cross for everyone. "The grace of God is not for one group or another. It's for all," she told the board.

Afterward, the board talked more about core beliefs. Teaching the faith to another generation was a core belief for the First Church board members. Acknowledging this, they voted to fund the youth trip and looked forward to hearing about the event when the youth returned.

Emmaline understood Pastor Valerie's reflection on Galatians 3:28 and her conversation with Gina about Walt to be a spirit-filled coincidence. For Emmaline, both events affirmed her core belief that all are welcome at First Church.

As she continued working in the garden, Emmaline thought back to a recent workshop she had attended about family systems theory and leadership. The leader, Juan, had talked about how important it is for people to form and know their core beliefs. "We can only be well-differentiated people," he said, "if we act from our core beliefs."

Juan gave the example of generosity. "If I truly believe God in Jesus has redeemed me, then I want to give as God has given to me. An attitude of gratitude is a core belief for me. My giving of myself, my money, and my time all goes back to this core belief that God has graciously claimed me, and now I have the opportunity to share with others. This sort of core belief helps me be clear as I respond to people. I remind myself that to be a well-differentiated person, I need to be clear, calm, and connected with others."

Juan's comments gave Emmaline insight into how Gina might respond to Walt. She decided to talk to Gina about the importance of core beliefs. Maybe Gina could have a conversation with Walt about her own—not to scold or attack him, but to let him know welcoming all people is at the center of her life in Jesus Christ. Maybe Walt would listen and even reflect on his core beliefs. Maybe he would reconsider his racist position. Maybe not. In the end, all Gina can do is be clear, calm, and connected.

- Think about your core beliefs. What is really at the center of your life?

- How do you talk about your core beliefs with others?

CHAPTER 6.

EVACUATING FROM RELATIONSHIPS

Cutoff

They saw him from a distance, and before he came near to them, they conspired to kill him. They said to one another, "Here comes this dreamer. Come now, let us kill him and throw him into one of the pits; then we shall say that a wild animal has devoured him, and we shall see what will become of his dreams." But when Reuben heard it, he delivered him out of their hands, saying, "Let us not take his life." Reuben said to them, "Shed no blood; throw him into this pit here in the wilderness, but lay no hand on him"—that he might rescue him out of their hand and restore him to his father. So when Joseph came to his brothers, they stripped him of his robe, the long robe with sleeves that he wore, and they took him and threw him into a pit. The pit was empty; there was no water in it.

Then they sat down to eat, and looking up they saw a caravan of Ishmaelites coming from Gilead, with their camels carrying gum, balm, and resin, on their way to carry it down to Egypt. Then Judah said to his brothers, "What profit is it if we kill our brother and conceal his blood? Come, let us sell him to the Ishmaelites and not lay our hands on him, for he is our brother, our own flesh." And his brothers agreed. When some Midianite traders passed by, they drew Joseph up, lifting him out of the pit, and sold him to the Ishmaelites for twenty pieces of silver. And they took Joseph to Egypt. . . .

. . . Realizing that their father was dead, Joseph's brothers said, "What if Joseph still bears a grudge against us and pays us back in full for all the wrong that we did to him?" So they approached Joseph, saying, "Your father gave this instruction before he died, 'Say to Joseph: I beg you, forgive the crime of your brothers and the wrong they did in harming you.' Now therefore please forgive the crime of the servants of the God of your father." Joseph wept when they spoke to him. Then his brothers also wept, fell down before him, and said, "We are here as your slaves." But Joseph said to them, "Do not be afraid! Am I in the place of God? Even though you intended to do harm to me, God intended it for good, in order to preserve a numerous people, as he is doing today. So have no fear; I myself will provide for you and your little ones." In this way he reassured them, speaking kindly to them. (Gen 37:18–28; 50:15–21)

If you live in a region known for hurricanes, you know governors often encourage their state's inhabitants to evacuate before potentially devastating storms. Sometimes they even make evacuation mandatory. The idea is that you will be safe from the storm if you leave early and keep far away from the worst of it.

Is it possible to evacuate from relationships like we do from storms?

There are other storms of nature from which you cannot evacuate, because there is no warning. Consider earthquakes—governors don't announce on TV a mandatory evacuation in advance of them. Forecasters can give us good advance warning of hurricanes with those famous spaghetti models, but not so with earthquakes—they arrive suddenly and without warning. One moment, you are asleep; the next, your bed is shaking you awake and your chest of drawers is sliding across the room. No spaghetti models. No warning. The earthquake is here.

Are relationships more like a hurricane or more like an earthquake?

***

Joan and Felipe and their twin sons were members of St. Lucia Church. Felipe had been elected to the governing board and served two terms. During the second two-year term, he was president of the congregation. He had some difficult times during his presidency, including a significant financial shortfall one year and the pastor's resignation shortly thereafter. It was a stressful and anxious time.

Like Felipe, Joan was a leader and deeply involved in the parish's life. She started a special group of four teams at St. Lucia to serve dinner to homeless people each Monday. The group opened the fellowship hall to anyone who needed a meal, no questions asked. Each team took one Monday night a month. For her efforts, the mayor had recognized Joan as an outstanding community leader. But it wasn't always easy. At times, there were not enough donations, or volunteers failed to show up and serve.

Joan and Felipe were present for worship almost every Sunday morning. Well, except for vacation or the Sunday after Thanksgiving, when they were still visiting family in another state. But these folks were core members and part of the key leadership at St. Lucia Church.

So, when another leader, Fred, noticed a change in their worship habits, he thought it was somewhat odd. Like forecasters warning of an impending hurricane, Fred noticed they were missing a Sunday or two and then returned—only to be missing again the following Sunday. It seemed they only came to worship when one of them was reading the lessons for the morning, or when one of the twins was an acolyte.

It troubled Fred to see this early warning that something was happening, so he went to Pastor Kathy to talk about it. "Pastor," Fred said, "have you noticed Joan and Felipe and their boys have become inconsistent worshippers? They are usually so faithful. Is there something going on you know about?"

"Wow," Pastor Kathy replied, "I must admit I hadn't noticed. Thanks for pointing it out. I'm not aware of any issues or problems. Maybe we both need to get in touch with them and see what's going on."

"Good idea," Fred said. "I've seen this happen with others in the past, and the next thing you know, they are gone. It would be devastating for St. Lucia to lose them. I will reach out to Felipe this week. Could you call Joan?"

Pastor Kathy agreed to catch up with Joan, and Fred called Felipe and arranged to meet Thursday morning for coffee. That day, as they talked, Fred gently asked about Felipe's family's faith journey and what was happening. Finally, Felipe said they were unhappy with the twins' Sunday school class. It had been an awful experience. Some Sundays, no one showed up to teach. Other Sundays, the teacher was poorly prepared and the kids got nothing out of class. The twins were complaining constantly, and he and Joan were worried about their sons' faith education, so they had been church-shopping to see if they could find a suitable church community with a stronger education program. They were anxious about how the boys were not getting what they felt they needed.

Fred was devastated. Just as he had thought, their inconsistent worship was an early warning of the coming hurricane. Felipe and Joan and the boys were about to leave St. Lucia.

Fred remembered how his adult Sunday school class had studied family systems theory. One of his important learnings from that study was the concept of a cutoff, when anxiety becomes so intense in a situation that people cut off from one another, distancing themselves. You often hear about children moving away from home and rarely, if ever, contacting their families. Just that morning, Fred had read a "Dear Auntie" newspaper advice column in which Auntie tried to resolve a cutoff that defined the relationship of a daughter with her parents.

Fred saw the same thing here. Joan and Felipe were anxious. They wanted the twins to learn the core beliefs of their faith so they could mature into faithful disciples. In their anxiety, Felipe and Joan thought the only way they could do this was to cut off from St. Lucia and find another congregation.

When Pastor Kathy and Fred met at the office a week later, Fred found Pastor Kathy had had a similar conversation with Joan. As they talked about what to do, Pastor Kathy reflected on the story of Joseph, a biblical story of a cutoff. Joseph's brothers cut off from him. They were anxious about his supposedly favored position with their father, Jacob, so they sold Joseph into slavery. The brothers saw this as a way to distance themselves from Joseph, to cut off from him. It was sudden—more like an earthquake than a hurricane. In an instant, the brothers put Joseph in the pit and sold him into slavery. It solved the family's tension and anxiety for a moment. As the story reminds us, a cutoff does not necessarily end the relationship.

Pastor Kathy pointed out how the story weaves quite a tapestry, until the family was starving in the famine and went to Egypt for food. There, they discovered Joseph was now in charge and held his family's future in his hands. Ultimately, the family was reunited, and Jacob later died and was buried.

Once again, the brothers were anxious. They were afraid Joseph would take revenge on them for what they had done to him years before. When they came to Joseph hoping he would not punish them, he forgave them and made the surprising statement that although they meant to harm him, God meant all this for good. Joseph assured his brothers he had forgiven them. Their cutoff was overcome by the grace of God.

Unfortunately, in the case of St. Lucia and Felipe and Joan, the result became a complete cutoff, as they were there one Sunday and gone the next. It was almost like an earthquake—abrupt and virtually unexpected. A few months later, a letter arrived from another church, asking to transfer the membership of Joan, Felipe, and the twins. The cutoff was complete.

Pastor Kathy and Fred both approached the board about the issue of education at St. Lucia. The leaders responded with a mission statement and vision for the next three years. They would develop a learning plan with educational goals for preschool through high school. They committed to recruit passionate teachers, not just warm bodies. Finally, the congregation would host quarterly intergenerational events.

Rather than react and try to chase down the family who had left, the leaders managed their anxiety and made a plan for the future. This avoided the temptation to spend time blaming one another for a failure, real or perceived.

In this situation, the leadership learned from the experience and made their congregation stronger.

It is worrisome when longtime faithful members leave. It is even more troubling when they have a valid reason for doing so. One common reaction is to track them down and "get them to come back." This rarely works. Another common reaction is to place blame, but getting stuck in the blame game means nothing changes. A less anxious leadership will allow time to process, try to contact the people who left to learn something from them, and focus on the future.

- When have you seen cutoff in your congregation?

- Have you ever dealt with anxiety in your family or congregation by distancing?

CHAPTER 7.

TRIANGLES ARE NOT JUST IN GEOMETRY CLASS

Triangling

And so, brothers and sisters, I could not speak to you as spiritual people, but rather as people of the flesh, as infants in Christ. I fed you with milk, not solid food, for you are not ready for solid food. Even now you are still not ready, for you are still of the flesh. For as long as there is jealousy and quarreling among you, are you not of the flesh, and behaving according to human inclinations? For when one says, "I belong to Paul," and another, "I belong to Apollos," are you not merely human?

What then is Apollos? What is Paul? Servants through whom you came to believe, as the Lord assigned to each. I planted, Apollos watered, but God gave the growth. So neither the one who plants nor the one who waters is anything, but only God who gives the growth. The one who plants and the one who waters have a common purpose, and each will receive wages according to the labor of each. For we are God's servants, working together; you are God's field, God's buildings. (1 Cor 3:1–9)

Who doesn't appreciate a lush green lawn? Deep down, nearly everyone wants a verdant expanse without even a hint of crabgrass or so much as a single dandelion or weed. Lester dreamed of such a lawn surrounding his home, because his own was far from perfection. It was thin in places, and some days it seemed as if everywhere Lester looked, he spotted another weed. With winter coming to an end, he knew this was the time to finally try to remedy that.

Lester talked about a green lawn so much, even his wife grew tired of it. "Why not just cover the lawn with concrete and paint it green? No fuss, no muss," she said to him one night. Lester was pretty sure she was kidding. No, this year, Lester planned to find a lawn care specialist who could fertilize, apply weed control, and do whatever it took to get the job done.

The next morning, as Lester left for work, he found an advertisement for Gary's Green Grass. Gary guaranteed green grass and a weed-free lawn, or your money back. Lester was so excited, he called Gary's Green Grass from work. He spoke on the phone to Gary himself, who gave Lester such a deal—a reasonable price and no contract required. Lester would pay for what he needed every four weeks or so, and he could quit anytime. Gary promised Lester would be getting a phone call from Frank, a lawn care specialist, the day before the first treatment. This would allow Lester to meet face-to-face with the specialist.

A week later, Lester received a text from Frank. He'd be there in two hours to meet Lester. This was not going to work for Lester, who had a meeting at work that would take most of the day. He couldn't miss it, not even for a greener lawn. Besides, he thought he would get a day's warning. He texted back to reschedule, but Frank responded it wasn't that simple because scheduling was done through the main office. Lester would have to wait, and he was not happy.

After work, Lester was still annoyed. He called the owner of the company. From Lester's perspective, Gary promised much and delivered little. The owner, as expected, apologized and promised Lester more notice when his appointment was rescheduled in the near future.

This little tale of Lester's quest for a greener lawn is also the story of the creation of emotional triangles. An emotional triangle forms when two parties become so anxious with one another that they seek out a third person to relieve the stress between them.

Let's begin with Lester and his lawn. The second party in our anxious relationship can be something other than a person. In this case, it was Lester's lawn, which he was anxious to fix. He brought in the third person in the triangle: the lawn care company owner. They worked out a deal and Lester's anxiety was temporarily reduced.

Then a new triangle formed between Lester, the lawn care specialist, and Lester's work commitments. When Frank, the lawn care specialist, did not give Lester enough warning, his anxiety rose and he lashed out. Frank tried to lower Lester's anxiety by bringing the scheduling office into the relationship, thereby distancing himself from Lester and his anger but creating a new triangle.

This was only a temporary fix, because Lester still felt anxious. Next, he escalated the situation and contacted the owner of the company to get Frank to show up and fix his lawn. Of course, the owner promised to fix things for Lester. This formed a new triangle between Frank, the lawn care specialist; Gary, the owner; and Lester. Even something as simple as fertilizing a lawn can create a system of several triangles.

Similar triangles sprouted up in the city of Corinth

among the early Christians. St. Paul wrote to them about their divisions. Anxious to compete to gain personal status, folks triangled themselves, St. Paul, and Apollos. As St. Paul wrote: "For when one says, 'I belong to Paul,' and another, 'I belong to Apollos,' are you not merely human?" (v. 4) Triangles formed between the people, Paul, and Apollos, depending on who presided at their baptism.

St. Paul broke down the triangles by noting how he and Apollos simply did their jobs. In St. Paul's metaphor, he planted and Apollos watered. St. Paul then pointed the Corinthian believers to God as the source of their growth. He encouraged them to stop their quibbling about who was better and focus instead on the growth God offered them. It wasn't "Apollos baptized me, so I am better than you," but opening themselves to the nourishment of God's word that would empower them to full maturity in Christ. But first they needed to de-triangulate.

***

Triangles can form in groups of people, even congregations. Elizabeth and Sue, for example, served on the education team at Sunny Place Church. They agreed the Sunday school program needed updating. Their team met to discuss it with lively debate—Elizabeth and Sue both held strong opinions, but theirs seemed to be at odds. This led to intense anxiety in the relationship between Elizabeth and Sue.

Wanting to decrease the tension between Sue and herself, Elizabeth made an appointment the next morning with Pastor Claudia. Elizabeth hoped Pastor Claudia would agree with her, convince Sue to be on her side, and thus reduce the anxiety in what was now a new triangle.

The first triangle was Elizabeth, Sue, and the new program plan. Now the new triangle was Pastor Claudia, Sue, and Elizabeth.

Fortunately, Pastor Claudia immediately recognized this triangle and suggested it would be best for Elizabeth to speak directly to Sue and work out their differences. Pastor Claudia did not take on their anxiety, and so immediately removed herself from the triangle.

Elizabeth was not happy the pastor refused to solve her problem and reduce her anxiety, so she went to the church council president and demanded the new program plan be placed on the agenda for the next council meeting. A new triangle formed.

If you were the council president, how would you respond? How many triangles can you detect now? Is there any chance to de-triangulate and have a new program plan to serve Sunny Place Church? Anytime two people share anxiety, there is a tendency to pull in a third person to take the side of one of them. We see this at times in almost all relationships. Sometimes it can be healthy—a couple constantly at odds with each other can often benefit from a therapist or counselor. A skilled counselor will offer guidance and conversation, while leaving the anxiety where it belongs: with the couple.

Triangles happen every time a customer service representative fails to give me what I want. My first move is to create a triangle by demanding to speak with a supervisor. In a way, I am ganging up on the customer service representative, hoping that by enlisting another person to my perspective, the representative will be forced to give me what I want.

Triangles form when two people bond over their shared opinions on everything from politics to musical styles. Pause to think about where this happens in your own family, work, and social relationships—whether these are antagonistic triangles or simply triangles of commonality.

The danger with triangles in relationships that really matter comes when primary relationships are destroyed and anxiety remains unresolved. Pastor Claudia knew the importance of the relationship between Elizabeth and Sue. Her goal was to get them to talk to each other, find common ground, and work together for the sake of the gospel.

As in every other group of people, there are triangles in the life of your congregation. Some of those simply exist, say, in the form of shared values. Other times, those triangles can be destructive. When enough destructive triangles are present, you can feel the anxiety in the community. This anxiety often keeps newcomers from engaging in the congregation. People have enough stress in their own lives; they generally don't want to join a church that adds to it.

One of the most misused verses in all of scripture is Matthew 18:20: "For where two or three are gathered in my name, I am there among them." These words from Jesus are generally quoted at sparsely attended church gatherings, but that is not the context about which this scripture was written. Instead, in this passage, Jesus tells us how to deal with sin between members of the church. The first step is to go to the person and speak directly to them. If that does not work, Jesus instructs us to bring another with us. The times when two or three gather are when people are confronting one another with sin. Talk about an anxious time! In those difficult moments, Jesus promises to be present with us. Jesus promises to be the one to take our anxiety and worry and give us his peace in return. Even in the midst of the most anxious triangles, Jesus is present.

- Where have you experienced triangles in your congregation?

- When have you pulled in a third person to fix a relationship?

CHAPTER 8.

THE THINGS WE INHERIT

Multigenerational Transmission

The Lord passed before him and proclaimed,

> "The Lord, the Lord,
> a God merciful and gracious,
> slow to anger,
> and abounding in steadfast love and faithfulness,
> keeping steadfast love for the thousandth
> generation,
> forgiving iniquity and transgression and sin,
> yet by no means clearing the guilty,
> but visiting the iniquity of the parents
> upon the children
> and the children's children,
> to the third and the fourth generation."

And Moses quickly bowed his head toward the earth and worshiped. He said, "If now I have found favor in your sight, O Lord, I pray, let the Lord go with us. Although this is a stiff-necked people, pardon our iniquity and our sin, and take us for your inheritance." (Exod 34:6–9)

During a congregational leadership board meeting, Pastor Phil interrupted Don to correct him on a point of fact. In the heat of the moment, it was important to Pastor

Phil that the facts be established. He didn't think—he just spoke up, cutting off Don in the process.

Three days later, the board president received an email from Don, copied to Pastor Phil. In part, it read, "I have never been so offended in all my days. Pastor Phil interrupted me and told everyone in the room I was lying. I do not know how I can ever go back to that church."

Pastor Phil reached out to Don, who was willing to meet. When Pastor Phil arrived, he said to Don, "I am sorry I interrupted you the way I did and I am sorry I offended you. It was never my intention and I am sorry if that was the outcome."

Don graciously accepted the pastor's apology and promised to return to the congregation's leadership board and to the church. They chatted for some time about the local high school sports teams and plans for midweek Lenten services at the church. Just as the pastor was about to leave, Don said, "There's just one more thing . . ."

And with that, Don handed Pastor Phil a letter he had recently received from his daughter. She wrote, "I cannot believe you continue to act the way you do. I have never been so hurt and offended by anyone's words in my entire life. I don't know if I can ever be in the same room with you again."

"How should I respond, Pastor?" Don asked.

"I would tell her you are sorry, you love her, and you are here for her whenever she is ready," Pastor Phil said.

Parents pass on all sorts of things to their children, both good and bad, often without realizing it. Don had no idea he had passed on the tradition of writing angry letters followed by cutting off behavior, but clearly he had done just that.

Churches are much the same as families. From one generation to another within the church, ways of being, acting, and living together are passed on. We call this multigenerational transmission. When the current pastor wants to lead a group from the church on a pilgrimage to the Holy Land, for example, the invitation will be better received in a congregation with a history of such travel. Even if it has been twenty years since the last trip, there is still a memory, an idea that this is who we are.

The book of Exodus tells us things are passed from one generation to the next:

> The Lord, the Lord,
> a God merciful and gracious,
> slow to anger,
> and abounding in steadfast love and faithfulness,
> keeping steadfast love for the thousandth generation,
> forgiving iniquity and transgression and sin,
> yet by no means clearing the guilty,
> but visiting the iniquity of the parents
> upon the children
> and the children's children,
> to the third and the fourth generation. (vv. 6–7)

God continues to forgive and love the people of Israel, although one generation's sins are learned by the next as they are passed along. Here is multigenerational transmission in the scriptures.

Knowing the past and understanding traditions can be helpful in planning for the future. Imagine trying to initiate a capital campaign in a congregation with a history of failed campaigns and broken promises. When a pot of money has been sitting unspent for ten years instead of being used for the intended new education wing, trying to raise funds for its construction will understandably be met with suspicion and distrust. When there is a past success upon which to build, it will likely take far less effort to make something a reality.

***

Joan was new to St. Stephen Church. In her previous congregation, she had helped run its food pantry. She had always found herself looking forward to the third Thursday of the month, when the pantry was open and those in need were given many sacks of groceries. Thinking about all the meals that could be cooked with the food fed her soul.

Joan had proposed to the board at St. Stephen Church that the congregation open a food pantry. She was shocked when her proposal fell flat. No one smiled. Some people looked down at the table. In the end, the board chair said, "I know you care about this, but we are not interested in trying the food pantry thing again."

Joan did not know that until five years ago there had been a food pantry at the church. The previous administrator, however, had appeared to use the pantry as his personal grocery store. The church could never prove anything, but in the end the prudent decision seemed to be to close the pantry.

This illustrates the emotionality often passed from one generation of leaders to the next. Clearly, the problems associated with the earlier try at having a food pantry at St. Stephen Church brought significant anxiety, which the leaders did not acknowledge and process openly. Consequently, Joan innocently walked right into this mire of anxiety when she suggested launching a food pantry.

It can be tempting to discount the influence of the past on a congregation. After all, membership changes and new people come into leadership roles. You might think that would change everything, but memories and the emotional process persist, and stories are handed down from one generation to another with the anxiety attached.

This does not mean churches cannot ever do anything new, but it does mean knowing your past can help predict which ministries might be met with joy and excitement and which might be met with downward glances. If leaders place the anxiety created by past events on the table and address it openly, a healthier response will allow leaders to move on to new possibilities.

Every congregation has had times of success, when people were energized and engaged. Use past stories of success and excitement to inspire people for the future. Knowing where you have been can help you plan for the future.

What have you inherited from the saints who have gone before you? Where has there been energy and excitement? Where have there been challenges and difficulties you were not able to overcome?

***

Pastor Jill was new to St. John Church. The first thing she noticed in the sanctuary was the pastor's chair near the altar looked like a throne. She was not thrilled. During her first months at the new church, she held a series of get-to-know-you gatherings. At one event, she learned the chair was an inheritance from a congregation that had closed and merged with the current church. Pastor Jill chose to use it, even though it was not her preference. Honoring the past allowed her to move the congregation forward in important ways.

Who are some of the older members of the congregation who have longer memories? When might members of the leadership board interview some of those folks about the successes and failures of the past? You can certainly do new things and find ministry opportunities, even when there have been setbacks in the past. Knowing about those setbacks, however, makes it easier to anticipate anxiety and overcome repeat setbacks.

What are the stories about the congregation people like to retell? Which biblical stories seem to resonate best with your people? This can also be a way of finding those "because we've always done it that way" traditions.

***

Pastor Bill had just arrived home after worship on the second Sunday in May when the phone rang. "Pastor, what happened?" a member of his congregation asked. "Why weren't there flowers for all the mothers at church this morning?"

This was Pastor Bill's first Mother's Day at this church. He had no idea this church had a tradition of giving flowers to mothers. Later, in discussion with the leadership board, he asked who would get a flower. (Moms, of course.) Then he asked specifically *which* moms. Mothers of young children? (Yes.) Mothers with adult children? (Yes.) Mothers whose children had all died? Mothers who had given up children for adoption? Mothers who had miscarried and had no living children? The leadership board suddenly had a new and deeper understanding of motherhood and the complexities involved in something as seemingly simple as giving flowers to moms on Mother's Day.

The forgotten flowers created an opportunity to talk more deeply about mothers and motherhood and how the church could unintentionally hurt people. With this understanding, the leadership board spent the rest of its meeting reflecting on other innocuous traditions of theirs that could do more harm than good. They even reflected on some of the common words intended to help but that often do not, such as, "God never gives you more than you can handle."

Knowing your past helps you prepare for the future. Whether we realize it or not, congregational memory and the emotionality attached to it shapes what happens in the present and in the future.

- What stories have been passed from previous leaders to you?

- How do these memories carry anxiety that still influences decisions by your leaders?

CHAPTER 9.

WHO STOLE MY PEW?

Nuclear Family Emotional System

> Then little children were being brought to him in order
> that he might lay his hands on them and pray. The disciples
> spoke sternly to those who brought them, but Jesus said,
> "Let the little children come to me and do not stop them, for
> it is to such as these that the kingdom of heaven belongs."
> And he laid his hands on them and went on his way. (Matt
> 19:13–15)

Helen walked into church and could not believe her eyes.
For years, she had been sitting on the inside of the last
pew on the far side of the sanctuary. This Sunday, her pew
and the one in front of it were simply gone. Removed.
In their place was a carpet decorated with what looked
like roads and buildings. In the middle of the carpet was
a basket filled with toy cars. To one side was a small table
and chairs, with coloring books and crayons.

Helen spun on her heel and headed right for the
pastor's office. "Where is my seat?" she demanded.

Pastor John had expected this. Because Helen had spent
the winter in Florida, she had not been around for the
discussions about adding a children's section at the back
of the sanctuary. He was certain she would have voiced

a strong opinion on the matter had she been there. Now her opinion was amplified because this was the first she learned of the change.

"We've had a number of families with young children join recently," Pastor John said, "and we thought this might be a way to help them be together with their children for worship."

Helen was unmoved. "I have been a member of this church for thirty-six years. A couple new people come and suddenly you have to change everything and cater to them? This is outrageous."

Everybody likes the idea of new people coming into the church. Everybody says they want the church to grow. Of course, this is often said in the context of needing more money to pay the bills. What is often forgotten is that new people bring with them new ideas and new needs.

Helen may have been particularly vocal, but she was far from the only one who was less than thrilled by the changes. Change is difficult and uncomfortable. Change means adapting and adjusting to new things. If it felt the same and were not at all uncomfortable, it would not be change.

During times of change, it is especially important for a church to be sure about its mission and direction. If we say we are a welcoming congregation and understand part of our mission as welcoming all who enter our doors and worship with us, then it fits to make changes to help small children and others feel welcome.

Helen and others needed to be reminded part of the church's mission statement is "welcoming all in Christ's name." The change in the seating in the nave was prompted by leadership recognizing that younger families with children were visiting and joining more often and would benefit from a dedicated space for their children in the sanctuary. "All are welcome" means being willing to make changes, even when these changes are inconvenient.

Having a clear mission statement in place guides leaders as they make decisions, such as the change in the worship area's seating. They are not making changes on a whim or to satisfy a couple loud voices; their decisions are based on what they understand the congregation's mission to be.

***

During a congregational meeting at St. Matthew, people were discussing a motion to remove age restrictions on who could receive communion. Some people remembered when you had to be confirmed before you could receive communion. Then, later, you had to be in fifth grade to commune. Fifth graders would go through a special class for a few Sundays, and on Reformation Sunday at the end of October, they would receive first communion. It was a beloved tradition.

Now someone had proposed to do away with all that. Their proposal was to remove all restrictions, and when the pastor, the parents, and the child agreed the child was ready to commune, then the child would be welcome at the table. Conversation and learning would be a part of the process as the child prepared. There would be no age restriction.

For many people, this proposed change was just one thing too many. People lined up at the microphone to express their displeasure and disagreement. Emotions ran high and voices rose.

Then Ulrike stepped up to the microphone. Ulrike was a charter member of the congregation. She was in her eighties and her hair was pure white. "I have been a member here since my children were toddlers, and you are right that we have always had restrictions on who could commune. I had to be confirmed before I could. It will feel strange and uncomfortable for a while to see three-year-old children receiving communion, but after listening to the discussion and reflecting on the theological issues, I know it is the right thing to do. That's why I am voting in favor of this. I may be uncomfortable with it, but we need this change."

Ulrike voiced what everyone was feeling. She owned her discomfort but refused to let it hold everything back. For the good of everyone, she was willing to be uncomfortable for a time. What a gift to her congregation!

Unfortunately, things do not always work out this way. People become uncomfortable with a new idea, a new way of doing things, some sort of change. Of course, it's uncomfortable—everything new is at first. This is why rental cars can be challenging. You rarely know exactly which car you are going to get, and every car is set up differently. On one, you push the lever up for the windshield wipers to do a single swipe. On another, you push the lever down. Thanks be to God for the gift of the little arrow next to the fuel gauge that lets you know which side the gas tank is on before you pull up to the pump!

We do not always have those little indicators to make things easier in the rest of life, so we become anxious. One reality is that anxiety has no boundaries, and it is cumulative. This means anxiety at work plus anxiety at home add up. That's why, in itself, a change at church might not be such a big deal. But along with all the other changes and stresses in life, it can be the last straw. Each of us can only cope with so much anxiety, and then we react.

Many people feel church is the safest place to act out. They cannot yell at their boss and still keep their job. They cannot treat their spouse or children poorly, or their home life will be miserable. Life at church, though—that's another story, they think. Good Christians are supposed to love each other no matter what, so they feel relatively safe acting out their anxieties on the assumption that folks will love them regardless. This is one reason why being part of the leadership in the church can be even more challenging than being a leader in a work setting. You cannot fire difficult members. People bring their reactivity with them to church.

Being aware of this can make all the difference. It can be difficult, but faithful leaders do not take every criticism or challenge personally. Faithful leaders have to manage their own anxiety and carefully respond rather than react to the situation at hand. Knowing the people involved can make all the difference.

***

James was furious about the new praise service that had replaced his preferred traditional service at 9:00 a.m. on Sunday mornings. Right after worship one Sunday, he found Sue, the congregation board president, and he let her have it. He raised his voice loud enough for everyone to hear.

As Sue listened, she thought about James and his life as

of late. She knew a mere three weeks ago, James's mother had died and he had been the one to make all the decisions, while his two siblings came into town after the fact and complained about his choices. Sue also knew the company James worked for was going through yet another reorganization and James might lose his job. With this in mind, she heard his complaints differently.

Instead of yelling back, Sue was calm. She briefly explained how the church leaders had reached the decision to change the Sunday morning schedule. She acknowledged not everyone would be happy with the changes. Sue also asked James how he was doing since his mother's death, then she reminded him of how much everyone wanted new people to become part of the church and how new people inevitably bring changes.

James did not leave their discussion completely satisfied, but Sue felt better about the encounter. She was able to see James as a whole person, rather than someone who is simply complaining again. Sue remained calm, was clear about the reason for the change, and remained connected with James. Leadership is all about being calm, clear, and connected with folks when anxiety rises in the group.

Listen to this story about Jesus:

As he was setting out on a journey, a man ran up and knelt before him, and asked him, "Good teacher, what must I do to inherit eternal life?" Jesus said to him, "Why do you call me good? No one is good but God alone. You know the commandments: 'You shall not murder; you shall not commit adultery; you shall not steal; you shall not bear false witness; you shall not defraud; honor your father and mother.'" He said to him, "Teacher, I have kept all these since my youth." Jesus, looking at him, loved him and said, "You lack one thing; go, sell what you own, and give the money to the poor, and you will have treasure in heaven; then come, follow me." When he heard this, he was shocked and went away grieving, for he had many possessions. (Mark 10:17–22)

When Jesus encountered the rich young man, he saw him as a whole person as well. Jesus saw the young man with faithfulness and gifts to offer. He also saw the young man as one who had burdens and challenges. Jesus did not seem to expect the young man to follow him, but he was still able to love him.

Faithful leaders are likewise called to challenge *and* love. It is not easy, but being faithful is rarely so.

- When have you felt anxiety rise in multiple parts of your life and found it all too much?

- How can you manage your anxiety when others are reacting and treating you poorly?

CHAPTER 10.

ARE WE THERE YET?

Self-Differentiation

> The whole congregation of the Israelites complained against Moses and Aaron in the wilderness. The Israelites said to them, "If only we had died by the hand of the Lord in the land of Egypt, when we sat by the fleshpots and ate our fill of bread; for you have brought us out into this wilderness to kill this whole assembly with hunger." (Exod 16:2–3)

Leaving slavery in Egypt sounded like a great idea to the Israelites at the time. Crossing the Red Sea and running away from Pharaoh's army was certainly exciting. Now the Israelites were underway in the wilderness for a while and reality was setting in. They were traveling as nomads from one water source to the next. They had no clear destination in mind.

To make matters worse, the people were getting hungry and thirsty. The Judean wilderness was not like the oak and maple forests of the Appalachian Mountains of the eastern United States. This was a barren and empty place—sand and rocks, little vegetation, steep hillsides, and deep, narrow valleys. Bleak and desolate, it was a place you passed through on the way to better things.

This wilderness was where the Israelites spent forty years wandering, following their herds, searching for water and forage. Still at the beginning of their travels, they had no clear destination in mind and no clear goal. Is it any surprise they began to grumble?

Congregations set themselves up for a similar situation with depressing regularity. Have you ever heard a conversation like this?

"Pastor, how did the canned food drive go?"

"It was great!"

"How many cans of food were donated?"

"Lots!"

"That's great. What was our goal?"

"Not sure. We just hoped to get a bunch of food."

No one knows how much food was collected during the drive, nor what the goal was, and at the end, the people have no idea if this is something to celebrate or reevaluate. What if instead you had placed two empty grocery carts in front of the church with a specific list of the food pantry's needs? What if people had known the goal was to fill one cart with, say, peanut butter and the other with canned soup? Then when people see the carts filled to overflowing, it is clear this food drive was a success. Now people have something to celebrate.

When there are no clear goals or paths to follow, people become anxious. As anxiety rises, people will find things to worry about. Suddenly, the smallest things become incredibly important. Instead of focusing on ways to live out the gospel, a debate rages over whether to stand or kneel for communion, or what color the lounge's new carpet should be.

In the early 1970s, a church we know faced a crisis like this. When the new pastor arrived, people saw to their horror he had a thick beard. Concerned parties raised the issue at a leadership board meeting. How could this be allowed? A small—but, of course, vocal—group wanted to require that the pastor shave. The leadership board decided the thing to do was call a congregational meeting so everyone could weigh in on the pastor's beard. After much discussion, the congregation voted to allow the pastor to have a beard as he chose.

What a sad chapter in the life of the congregation! Of course, context matters. The early 1970s were the days when bearded hippies were busy protesting the Vietnam War and challenging many of the social norms people were accustomed to. Then came this pastor looking like one of those hippies. But rather than talk about their deeper anxiety—the war and the changes in society—the congregation members focused on the one thing staring them in the face: the pastor's beard.

You cannot make this kind of anxiety disappear. In every context and every time, changes are going on that bring anxiety into people's lives. Even if everything in the church were going smoothly, changes in the culture, changes at work, or changes at home would raise anxiety in people.

If you can't make anxiety go away, all that's left to do is respond to it and deal with it. This is the time for leaders to be calm, clear, and connected to the congregation. But to bring clarity to anxious times and to reduce anxious reactivity, leaders need to be well self-differentiated.

In the case of the wandering Israelites, all they wanted was a place for the night where there was water and food for themselves and their herds. Every day that ended without those things, they became anxious. They did not understand the time in the wilderness as an opportunity for them to acknowledge and practice their complete dependence on God. They did not see it as a chance to learn to trust God would always provide enough for everyone. No wonder they lashed out at Moses! Congregations can go for years wandering from one program to the next with no clear sense of direction or purpose. They may as well be wandering in the wilderness with the Israelites.

Faithful leaders will cast a compelling vision and point to a destination. This can start small, like filling grocery carts with food. That is only the beginning, but it is also good practice. A clear vision that fits the congregation's mission gives clarity, and this allows a church to be healthier.

Leaders cast such a vision by intentionally spending time in conversation about the congregation's future. It is all too easy for board meetings to become nothing but a time to report what happened last month and plan for what will happen next month. Add a quick report from the treasurer, and everyone can go home early. Planning for a longer time—say, three years—brings clarity and gives opportunities for folks to participate in the congregation's mission and ministry.

***

Grace Church received an unexpected bequest of nearly $500,000. There was much talk of ways to use the money for the good of the church, from paying off the mortgage to buying a pipe organ. In the end, the church chose to use a significant portion of the gift to replace the pews in the sanctuary with chairs.

Not everyone saw the merit in this plan, particularly

those who had wanted to pay off the mortgage. The board president explained the decision, saying, "We have talked about ways to make our worship space more inviting. We want people with walkers and wheelchairs to be able to navigate the space easily. We want to be more creative in worship to engage more people. Chairs allow us to reconfigure the space for dynamic worship services in a way that pews do not. We want our worship space to be welcoming."

This congregation has a vision of being more welcoming and being known for creative worship. Not everyone will agree on the means they chose to make that vision a reality, but it is difficult to argue with the vision. What church wouldn't want to be more welcoming? It's hard to make a case for being unwelcoming and boring.

***

Now as they went on their way, he entered a certain village, where a woman named Martha welcomed him into her home. She had a sister named Mary, who sat at the Lord's feet and listened to what he was saying. But Martha was distracted by her many tasks, so she came to him and asked, "Lord, do you not care that my sister has left me to do all the work by myself? Tell her then to help me." But the Lord answered her, "Martha, Martha, you are worried and distracted by many things; there is need of only one thing. Mary has chosen the better part, which will not be taken away from her." (Luke 10:38–42)

In this passage, Martha is anxious because she suddenly has unexpected guests in her home and has had it drummed into her all her life that when guests come to your home, you feed them. In her anxiety, she cannot see past this.

Faithful leadership will not change the reality of anxiety in people's lives. People will still find things to worry, argue, and complain about. Some—but not all—of those things might even have merit. Faithful leaders will remind the congregation "there is need of only one thing." For churches, this means faithfully proclaiming and living out the good news of Jesus. People will always be worried and distracted by many things, so leaders will need to point again and again to the larger mission of the kingdom and the promises of God.

- When have you seen anxiety arise and distract a congregation from the gospel?

- Toward what mission and vision does your leadership point your congregation?

CHAPTER 11.

STUCK IN A RUT

Nuclear Family Emotional System

For just as the body is one and has many members, and all the members of the body, though many, are one body, so it is with Christ. For in the one Spirit we were all baptized into one body—Jews or Greeks, slaves or free—and we were all made to drink of one Spirit.

Indeed, the body does not consist of one member but of many. If the foot would say, "Because I am not a hand, I do not belong to the body," that would not make it any less a part of the body. And if the ear would say, "Because I am not an eye, I do not belong to the body," that would not make it any less a part of the body. If the whole body were an eye, where would the hearing be? If the whole body were hearing, where would the sense of smell be? But as it is, God arranged the members in the body, each one of them, as he chose. If all were a single member, where would the body be? As it is, there are many members, yet one body. The eye cannot say to the hand, "I have no need of you," nor again the head to the feet, "I have no need of you." On the contrary, the members of the body that seem to be weaker are indispensable, and those members of the body that we think less honorable we clothe with greater honor, and our less respectable members are treated with greater respect; whereas our more respectable members do not need this. But God has so arranged the body, giving the greater honor to the inferior member, that there may be no dissension within the body, but the members may have the same care for one another. If one member suffers, all suffer together with it; if one member is honored, all rejoice together with it.

Now you are the body of Christ and individually members of it. (1 Cor 12:12–27)

It was just after 7:00 a.m. on a summer Sunday morning and Pastor Frank was turning into the church parking lot. In a little less than an hour, the first of two worship services would begin. He knew he would once again walk into a sanctuary that had the capacity to seat over two hundred people and there would be at most two dozen people in the pews. More likely, there would be fewer than twenty.

At the second service, well over one hundred people attended on a regular basis. The previous summer, he had tried combining the services, but those first service early birds refused to budge. They boycotted worship and withheld their offerings. Money had been tight throughout the fall because of it. So here he was, exhausted, and once more arriving about the time he should be getting out of bed so a handful of people could keep their precious routine.

It wasn't that Pastor Frank was lazy; it just all felt so futile. The sanctuary could easily accommodate everyone at both services at the same time, with room to grow. He also knew the chances for significant growth of an 8:00 a.m. worship service were slim to none, and Slim was likely on a bus headed south. And then there was the reality that following the first service, there would be at least an hour when he and the musician were the only ones in the building until the next service at 11:00 a.m.—all so a few people could check their box for worship that day and get to breakfast, just like they had always done.

This is the way things have always been, and they are not going to change. The folks at the early service are thinking only about themselves, their traditions, their habits, and their patterns. This is a congregation stuck in a rut and going nowhere because of it.

Leaders challenge members as part of their call to lead. Merely perpetuating the present results in a stagnant body of Christ. Without a mission or vision other than keeping things as they are, folks will begin to pick at issues just to have something to do. Failing to challenge a congregation results in a survival mentality, which does not serve the mission and ministry to which we are called.

In the excerpt from Corinthians, Paul reminds us no one is in this alone. We are all connected to one another as the body of Christ, just like the parts of our human body are connected. If the people from the 8:00 a.m. service were to begin to think of the whole church rather than just their little part it, they might see things differently. Doing that might mean some change on their part, and that would prove uncomfortable. They have no interest in discomfort.

Is your congregation stuck in a rut? If your annual planning primarily consists of changing the date for the same events every year, you might be. Sure, part of this is the reality of the patterns of the year. It doesn't make sense to put up harvest decorations in June. Still, if fewer and fewer people are engaged in those same old activities year after year, maybe it is time to try something new. Shake things up. Challenge folks to greater mission and ministry.

When individuals in the congregation focus on

themselves and what makes them happy and comfortable regardless of everyone else, those ruts are likely to become canyons. Rather than simply asking what worship times people in the congregation prefer, what if a different question were posed, such as, "What worship time would be most preferred by potential first-time visitors?" If one part of the congregation's mission is to share the good news of Jesus, then isn't this the most important question?

***

St. Thomas Church had had three services on Christmas Eve, at 5:00, 7:30, and 11:00 p.m., for more than forty years. There was once a time when extra chairs had to be brought in for the 11:00 p.m. service, but those days were long past. Looking at recent trends, the leadership board noticed the least well-attended was the 11:00 p.m. service. Yet a handful of extremely vocal people had organized their family Christmas traditions around that service. Any earlier, and there was no way they could attend.

In January, the board started discussing plans for the next Christmas Eve worship schedule, so there was plenty of time for conversation and they would not feel rushed. They realized the church could hold everyone if they combined the 7:30 and 11:00 p.m. services. If everyone came at the same time, the church would feel packed.

Still, it was not an easy decision. One member of the board lamented, "If we do away with the 11:00 p.m. service, it will be the first time in thirty-six years I won't be in church on Christmas Eve." Another said, "I just don't feel safe driving at night anymore, and when I get home after midnight, I am exhausted all day on Christmas." There were strong feelings on both sides of the issue.

The board spent the next couple months in conversation. This allowed time for people to think things through carefully. Finally, the board opted to offer two worship services the next Christmas: one at 5:00 p.m., with a focus on young children and families, and a second at 9:00 p.m. One board member said, "If nothing else, see how it goes. At least we tried to fill the place."

Making changes and getting out of ruts is not easy. The easy thing is to keep things the same. St. Thomas Church had a vision to make the church feel full on Christmas Eve. Unfortunately, offering three services was not going to accomplish that vision. Inevitably, there were people who felt slighted and left behind by the decision to cut one service and change the service times. But when the next Christmas Eve came, at the 9:00 p.m. service, more people were in worship at one time than had been in years. Some people missed out, but the place felt full. There was hope the next year would be even better.

Anxiety can lead to us keep things the same for the sake of peace, even at the cost of growth. People are creatures of habit, and new things can feel uncomfortable and awkward. Faithful leaders will manage their own anxiety and focus on clear and measurable goals, even if it means some hard feelings from people who disagree. Well-differentiated leaders will challenge a congregation to grow.

Throughout the process, it is essential to frame the question in a way that points toward the church's mission and its vision for the future. If the question in September is "What fellowship event should we hold in October?" chances are the answer will be something along the lines of "How about what we did last year?" Instead, look ahead and ask questions such as "How can we engage the community around us?" or "What worship times would the people in the community be most likely to attend?"

If the leadership board is focused on the question "How can we keep the people here happy?" you can be sure not much will change. But what if it were to ask, "How can we challenge the people of the congregation to live out the good news of Jesus?" or "What would be so exciting that people would feel compelled to tell others?"

- When have you had to make changes that were not received with joy by everyone involved?

- As a leader in your congregation, what challenges are needed?

CHAPTER 12.

HAS YOUR CHURCH BEEN VACCINATED?

Nuclear Family Emotional System

The whole congregation of the Israelites set out from Elim; and Israel came to the wilderness of Sin, which is between Elim and Sinai, on the fifteenth day of the second month after they had departed from the land of Egypt. The whole congregation of the Israelites complained against Moses and Aaron in the wilderness. The Israelites said to them, "If only we had died by the hand of the Lord in the land of Egypt, when we sat by the fleshpots and ate our fill of bread; for you have brought us out into this wilderness to kill this whole assembly with hunger." (Exod 16:1–3)

Midway Church had been in crisis mode for some time. There was conflict between the pastor and the leadership board. There was conflict between the pastor and the musician. Conflict was everywhere you turned.

So Midway Church brought in consultants to help. Something had to be done before the church completely imploded. The consultants followed a process, meeting with many people in the congregation, sometimes one on one, sometimes in groups. Eventually, they produced a report with their findings and suggestions for the congregation.

To present the consultants' report to the entire congregation at one time, the board called a congregational meeting and gave everyone a paper copy. The lead consultant said he would read one paragraph at a time, then pause for comments. It seemed like a good plan, but it did not work.

The people at the meeting were so anxious that it was rare for the consultant to read even one sentence, let alone a paragraph, uninterrupted. People did not bother raising their hands; they just shouted over the consultant and over one another. Never once did someone in the congregation interject to suggest they offer the consultant the respect of allowing him to read each paragraph before they commented.

In the end, the consultant's recommendations were largely ignored, and by fall, the board had asked the pastor to resign. The board invited the pastor to stay on through Christmas, however, because it did not want to worry about who would preach on Christmas Eve.

This is a congregation without an immune system. It does not have someone to remind it how to behave and how to stay healthy. What a difference it would have made if one member had stood up, apologized to the consultant, and asked everyone to follow the agreed-upon rules.

In a healthy congregation, there are individuals who function as white blood cells do in the human body to fight infections. Sometimes these cells produce antibodies to fight the bacteria. Other times, the cells surround and overwhelm an infection, thus providing a protective shield for the body. Anxiety can spread like an infection, and if left unchecked, it can contaminate everyone in the congregation. In congregations, things such as anonymous complaints, unhealthy rumors, gossip, and triangles are all signs of anxiety.

In the passage from Exodus, we can see the anxious infection has spread throughout the people—"the whole congregation of the Israelites complained against Moses and Aaron" (v. 2). No one was free from the anxiety. Of course, there was reason for their concern: they wanted to survive. They were traveling through an unfamiliar wilderness with their families and herds and everything they owned. Without water, they would die. The challenge was that unchecked anxiety trapped them into making black-and-white distinctions rather than learning to live with the gray. In this case, the Israelites suggested that because they did not die in Egypt, they would die in the wilderness. They thought there was no hope.

Congregations in times of crisis can develop the same sort of thinking. "Either this problem gets fixed immediately, or our church will die," they say. Calls go out to the judicatory staff, "We are going to close next Sunday if you do not come right now!" When the response is not immediate, the anxiety grows.

Being an immune system in a congregation means refusing to take on another's anxiety. It means remaining calm, or at least less anxious, when voices are raised. It means listening to others but not necessarily agreeing with everything they suggest. Chances are the church will not be closing within the month, no matter how grave the situation appears.

This is why a clear and well-written mission statement is helpful. With a clear statement, leaders can point to a congregation's mission when anxiety rises and refocus on the congregation's larger purpose rather than its immediate anxiety. Annual visions for ministry and service that fulfill the congregation's mission help reduce anxiety and its symptoms. A healthy immune system needs both a clear mission statement and a vision for ministry.

***

Hank had been the chair of the committee the congregation had formed when it was searching for a new musician and choir director. Hank knew music was vital to the congregation's worship. Most of the folks tolerated average sermons, but bad music leadership brought out immediate and intense complaints.

Early on in the search process, this committee had found a candidate who seemed like the perfect fit for their congregation. The musician could play both piano and organ, and he was known as a gifted choir director. Rather than spending lots of time interviewing and auditioning multiple candidates, the committee had chosen to move forward with him.

Most of the congregation was fine with this choice, but not everyone. John was strongly opposed. He was furious when he read the announcement of the appointment of the new musician and choir director in the church email blast. He didn't care if this was the best possible candidate; he did not understand how they could make such an important decision without interviewing several people. The congregation's music was too important. How could they do this?

John arrived early at church the next Sunday and went directly to Hank. "I know you are the chair of the committee that hired this new organist," he said. "How could you do that without talking with anyone else? How could you not hear anyone else play even a note?" John was beside himself.

Hank took a slow breath. "In our conversations as a committee," Hank said, "we talked about how few highly qualified musicians there are right now. With so few choices, once we had a gifted person who was interested in the job, we simply had to move forward. We are content with our decision."

John was not satisfied. The following two Sundays, he repeatedly demanded an explanation from Hank. After a couple weeks of repeating the same response, Hank was done. "You keep asking the same question. You already know my answer and it is not going to change," Hank said to John one Sunday. "I am sorry you are not satisfied with my response, but I am thrilled with the musician who is coming to our church. You need to know I dread coming to church and having to answer the same question from you every week. I am never having this conversation with you again."

Hank chose to function as an immune system for the congregation. He stayed connected to John and listened to his concerns, but he was not willing to allow John to abuse him. Hank told John, in essence, "This is how our church is choosing to operate in this situation. I know you do not like it. You have made that clear. You can either accept the decision or go on your way, but you cannot be abusive."

Every congregation needs people to function in this way. An immune system reflects the community's shared values. It is best if this role is filled by someone other than the pastor. When laypeople step forward, it makes it clear this is not just the way the pastor wants things to be.

Interestingly, sometimes the people who think they have the smallest voice can make the biggest difference. Imagine a hostile congregational meeting. People are raising their voices. What would happen if one of the oldest members of the congregation stood up and reminded people to speak to one another in love?

For a disease to take hold, it needs room to grow and expand. This is the same for anxiety. One anxious person writes a letter to the leadership team about all the "unnecessary" changes in the church since the new pastor arrived. When that person takes the letter around to find additional signatories, if no one else signs on, the original letter writer's anxiety will often fade naturally. The exact opposite can happen when a half dozen others add their name to the letter. Now a crisis is brewing, even in the absence of credible concerns.

There are responsible ways to voice concerns in the life of a congregation—letter-writing campaigns, gossip, and more are not among them. The congregation needs people who encourage others to communicate directly when problems arise. These are the folks who make up the congregation's immune system. Without them, the congregation may well flounder in a sea of anxiety.

- When have you functioned as the immune system in an organization?

- Who can you identify as part of the immune system in your congregation?

CHAPTER 13.

SECRETS KILL

Nuclear Family Emotional System

> Meanwhile, when the crowd gathered by the thousands so that they trampled on one another, he began to speak first to his disciples, "Beware of the yeast of the Pharisees, that is, their hypocrisy. Nothing is covered up that will not be uncovered, and nothing secret that will not become known. Therefore, whatever you have said in the dark will be heard in the light, and what you have whispered behind closed doors will be proclaimed from the housetops." (Luke 12:1–3)

People were grumbling and unhappy. Things were going poorly. Clearly, there were issues with the pastor, so the executive committee called a meeting with him. One member of the executive committee owned a small business and another worked in human resources, so they both knew about the employment law in their state. They were very clear on one thing: conversations about employment issues, like the one between the executive committee and the pastor, are to be kept confidential. No one, not even the pastor, could share with the congregation what was discussed.

Still, everyone at St. John Church knew there had been a meeting. They knew there were problems. They wondered what the meeting was about. What had the pastor done? Was it something illegal? Had he stolen money from the church? Had he made a sexist comment to someone? Everyone hoped and prayed it had nothing to do with sex. The executive committee kept quiet, but the rumors grew and grew.

This is a reminder of the destructive power of secrets, especially in groups of people. When something goes wrong, all too often people's first inclination is to cover it up or hide it, hoping this bad thing will simply go away and everything will go back to normal. This rarely works.

In 1974, articles of impeachment were drawn up to remove then President Richard Nixon from office. The articles centered on three charges: obstruction of justice, abuse of power, and contempt of Congress. How interesting that, more than the crimes themselves, Nixon was charged for actions he took to try to cover up or hide the crimes. This should not be surprising. It is common for the cover-up to get you in as much trouble as the crime itself. Still, people continue to try to hide their deeds, thinking maybe this time they will get away with it.

Within a church community, secrets can be particularly destructive. Congregations are intended to be safe spaces where you are surrounded by people you can trust. When there are secrets, there is no trust.

It is important to note the difference between secrets and keeping things confidential. If the financial giving records of individuals are so secret that only one person has knowledge of and access to them, there is a problem. For example, if this person who keeps the information secret dies suddenly, no one will be able to audit accounts, provide IRS statements, and more. So, while several people, including the pastor, treasurer, and one or two others might have access to giving records, they will keep these confidential and not share their knowledge with others. In counseling and confessional conversations, pastors will promise to keep what is said confidential, unless it involves a danger to one's self or others. This is the important distinction between secrecy and confidentiality.

*∗∗

Holy Cross Church was finally set to pay off its mortgage. For years, the debt had been hanging over the congregation. With the mortgage paid off, more than $40,000 a year would be freed up in the budget. As the board discussed plans for the coming year, Rodrigo suggested they not tell the congregation about the mortgage. "If people know we don't have any debt, they will stop giving," he said.

Rodrigo was not alone in his anxiety. On the other hand, if the board chose to keep this information secret, when it did finally come out—and it would!—how much trust would people have in the board? If there was no trust in their leadership, generosity would surely suffer.

After some discussion, Beth spoke up. "For years, we have been talking about hosting a seminary intern. With that $40,000 and a little more, we just might be able to do that. What if we tell the people the mortgage is paid in full and this gives us a chance to use our offerings for a powerful new ministry?" Heads nodded in agreement before Beth had even finished speaking. There was a new energy in the room. People loved the idea of using the money for ministry.

Leaders know secrets kill open and healthy communication. When this happens, secrets actually kill relationships, bringing new issues into a congregation and complicating the issues that initiated the secrets. Secrets create division; they splinter a congregation. There are those who are in on the secret, and others who are on the outside. The resulting divisions isolate people from one another. Secrets can create these divisions without folks even noticing or knowing why.

Healthy leaders will truthfully and openly place issues on the table so the congregation can address them. This can be a difficult moment. It is not easy to confront issues that might bring controversy and disagreement. Putting issues on the table, however, means the anxiety surrounding them will decrease after the initial reaction. This is how healthy leaders handle difficult situations.

If issues are hidden, that secrecy will lead to broken relationships. When the secrets are revealed—and they will be!—folks will feel they can no longer trust leaders. They will be distant from and wary of what the leaders do in the future. Thus, members' ability to focus on future issues and opportunities will be blurred by the history of secrets.

Still, bad news raises anxiety, and often people hope if they ignore it, the bad news will simply go away. Some folks call this living on the river of "de Nile" (denial). It's a cute way to bring up leaders' tendency to try to ignore something that obviously needs their attention.

Here is an example: Bethel Church's parking lot was crumbling to bits. It was obvious to everyone. Then, one day, the local city government sent the church a letter informing them that if the parking lot was not repaired in a timely fashion, the city would be forced to condemn it and forbid anyone from parking on it. Christi, the board president, saw the letter and suggested they ignore it. The second letter from the city was more stern and included a fairly tight time frame for repairs. That letter was ignored as well.

Finally, one Sunday morning, the congregation learned of the situation for the very first time when they arrived to find yellow plastic tape cordoning off the parking lot and a notice on the front door declaring the lot condemned until the situation was remedied. That was bad enough, but once people learned the president had kept these letters secret, they were furious. Denial did not work at Bethel Church.

Imagine the difference if the information had been shared from the beginning. The news would have been painful but not destructive. The members of the congregation would not have lost trust in the leadership. It could even have been presented as a challenge they could face together, an obstacle to overcome, and finally an achievement to celebrate. Instead, the congregation was thrown into turmoil—attendance declined, giving dropped, and the parking lot repairs were paid for by refinancing the mortgage, pleasing no one. Denial is not a good option for leaders.

There was an additional unhealthy response to the parking lot problems at Bethel Church. When the congregation learned about the problem and how the leadership had denied its existence, Christi decided the pastor was at fault. Remember, it was Christi, the board president, who had encouraged the secret, the denial. Now, Christi had started a campaign to blame the pastor. She called, texted, and emailed her friends, drumming up the idea that the pastor should have opposed the leadership and made an issue of the parking lot. As Christi saw it, he was really the one at fault. It was classic scapegoating and an unhealthy attempt to shift the responsibility for poor leadership to the pastor from the board—specifically her, its president.

Like secrets and denial, scapegoating is another unhealthy attempt to manage conflict. Clear communication outlining the parking lot issue would have served Bethel Church better. There may have been a short time of discomfort, but in the long run, such leadership would have been much healthier.

- How do you distinguish between secrecy and confidentiality?

- What secrets are hiding in your congregation?

CHAPTER 14.

WHEN HELPING IS NOT

Self-Differentiation

On their return, the apostles told Jesus all they had done. He took them with him and withdrew privately to a city called Bethsaida. When the crowds found out about it, they followed him, and he welcomed them, and spoke to them about the kingdom of God, and healed those who needed to be cured.

The day was drawing to a close, and the twelve came to him and said, "Send the crowd away so that they may go into the surrounding villages and countryside, to lodge and get provisions, for we are here in a deserted place." But he said to them, "You give them something to eat." They said, "We have no more than five loaves and two fish—unless we are to go and buy food for all these people." For there were about five thousand men. And he said to his disciples, "Make them sit down in groups of about fifty each." They did so and made them all sit down. And taking the five loaves and the two fish, he looked up to heaven, and blessed and broke them, and gave them to the disciples to set before the crowd. And all ate and were filled. What was left over was gathered up, twelve baskets of broken pieces. (Luke 9:10–17)

Nativity Church wanted to make a difference in the lives of impoverished people. The church also wanted to make a big splash. So members of the congregation rented a couple vans and drove all over town to find people in need. Some of the people were homeless, others lived in rental properties, but none of them had many resources. These were people in need of some good, old Christian charity.

The church quickly filled up its vans and dropped off the people at a grocery store, inviting the people to fill their carts with groceries. Everyone was having a great time. They talked about meal planning and feasts for their families. The church paid for the groceries, then the church members hopped into the vans and their cars and drove off. Job well done.

Except the people from the church did not realize transportation is a great challenge for people in poverty. Now these couple dozen folks were stranded miles from home with more groceries than they could carry.

Helping people is not always easy. Looking from the outside, the problem seemed simple: people are hungry, so take them to the store and buy them food. Because many of the people from the church had owned a car from the time they were teenagers, it never occurred to them that an adult might not own one. They never considered the huge financial barriers to car ownership, from licensing to registering to insuring, let alone purchasing. In the end, bags of groceries were left to spoil in the sun and a few dozen resentful people from the poor side of town were stranded.

A well-differentiated person takes time to reflect, think through the situation, and be clear about what is needed. Yes, they will also be calm and connected with others, but the key is to use the part of their brain that allows them to think through the response they are making to an anxious situation.

The folks at Nativity Church were anxious. They wanted to help. Their desire was driven by an emotional process that prompts a person to fight, take flight, freeze, or nurture, much like a reptile does. This survival part of the brain is important, but the reactivity that emanates from it when we are highly anxious does not always serve us well.

The folks at Nativity Church needed to step back and not be reactive. Pausing to consider all the situation's possibilities and ramifications would have helped them realize the folks they were helping needed to get home after shopping. Arrangements needed to be made.

Such emotional processes can also enter our relationships at home. Here is the story of Tim and Drew, father and son. Tim was frustrated. He and his five-year-old son, Drew, were running late for a doctor's appointment. The morning had gotten away from them, and now young Drew was trying to tie his shoes. After a half dozen attempts, Tim swooped in, tied his son's shoes, scooped him up, and got him in the car. They made the appointment just in time. The next time Tim started to rush him, Drew didn't even try tying his shoes. He just sat there and said, "Dad, you do it." Drew learned if he just sat there, his dad would tie his shoes for him. It seemed like a good idea to Drew, but Tim was not impressed.

Here was an anxious father who wanted to be on time for their appointment. He jumped in to fix things and signaled to his son that if he just waited, Dad would do it for him. In family systems theory, we call this a boundary problem. When Dad was anxious and fixed things himself, he crossed a boundary, not allowing Drew to be independent or to care for himself in this situation. Keeping healthy boundaries means being attentive to where I end and you begin so we do not try to control the other person.

Being well-differentiated and keeping healthy boundaries makes helping different than enabling. It is one thing to bring a few meals to someone after surgery. It is another to find you are expected to provide daily meals in perpetuity. Rather than making someone dependent on you, it might be more appropriate to connect them with organizations and resources designed to provide them with long-term help. The short-term challenge is that this can be a painful path because it may well appear to be a hard-hearted choice.

Often, doing too much for others has more to do with our own anxiety than anything else. Fixing the presenting issue makes things easier for us. Tim tied his son's shoes because he was anxious about getting to an appointment on time. This works in the short term, but like all parents, Tim was looking forward to the day when his child could tie his own shoes and wouldn't need a parent to do everything for him.

It can be tempting to run around and take care of everything so it gets done just right, but in the long term, that creates a culture of dependency. As soon as that person who did everything goes away, there is a void to fill. Poor boundaries and a lack of self-differentiation lead to dependency.

In the reading from Luke at the beginning of this chapter, Jesus instructed the disciples, saying, "You give them something to eat" (v. 13). Everyone needs food and everyone needs to eat daily. Emergency food aid remains a sad necessity, even in some of the wealthiest countries in the world. Still, emergency food aid does not solve the problem of hunger. In the gospel, the need was short-term and immediate because the crowds were far from home.

This is not the case for people who patron modern-day food pantries. These are folks with chronic food insecurity, often combined with health and employment challenges. Daily food is one step, but the need for longer-term solutions for housing, health care, and employment complicate the situation. This is the challenge for modern followers of Jesus who seek to both feed people each day and provide people with what they need so they have the resources to feed themselves.

***

Pastor Bill was finishing up writing his sermon and was about to head home when a woman he did not know arrived with her six-year-old daughter in tow. They needed money for a hotel room for the night. Pastor Bill had heard stories like hers before and had worked to cultivate a relationship with the people who ran the local family shelter. He knew it was a safe space with food and social workers who could connect people with the needed services and resources that could help them move out of homelessness.

Yet when he suggested the shelter to the woman, she responded with a litany of excuses. She knew they were all the same. She had had a bad experience in a different shelter. She just needed the money for one night in a hotel.

Pastor Bill wanted to be faithful and generous. Pastor Bill also knew one night in a hotel would not change the future for this woman and her daughter. Their best option was the local shelter and the help of the hardworking and knowledgeable social workers they would find there.

- What would you do if you were Pastor Bill? How would you respond if the woman kept refusing to go to the shelter?

- Can you think of a time you helped too much and made things worse in the long term?

CHAPTER 15.

WHERE IS GOD IN THIS?

Emotional Process in Society

> Just then, a lawyer stood up to test Jesus. "Teacher," he said, "what must I do to inherit eternal life?" Jesus said to him, "What is written in the law? What do you read there?" He answered, "You shall love the Lord your God with all your heart, and with all your soul, and with all your strength, and with all your mind; and your neighbor as yourself." And he said to him, "You have given the right answer; do this, and you will live."
>
> But, wanting to justify himself, he asked Jesus, "And who is my neighbor?" (Luke 10:25–29)

In the early 1960s, the national church parachuted a pastor into a new suburban community growing outside Detroit. The pastor did not actually jump out of an airplane, but he might as well have. Pastor Jim was sent alone to start a new church by literally knocking on doors and inviting people to church.

In those days, new churches were started by sending a solo pastor to a growing community with a stack of brochures and enough funds to rent some space and get things going. The goal was for the congregation to have its first building unit be complete and financially self-sustaining within three to four years.

When Pastor Jim looked down the long rows of homes in the community, he felt confident and hopeful. His denomination had given him the title Mission Developer and instructed him in the fine art of meeting people on their doorsteps. He was also confident because he could safely assume the vast majority of homes were inhabited by people with Christian backgrounds.

Pastor Jim chose the name St. James Church for the congregation. Soon, it was officially organized and up and running. The church grew quickly, and over the decades it replaced pastors, added new staff, and built on to the building. The church stabilized and became a faithful presence in the community.

The community, however, continued to change. The schools' excellent reputation drew many engineers and medical professionals to the community. Many of these people were not born in America and did not have a Christian background. It was no longer the case that nearly all the community's homes were occupied by people with Christian backgrounds. It was not just the difference between Roman Catholics and Protestants; the community now included people who were Hindu, Muslim, and Buddhist.

These changes were a steady source of concern for some members of the congregation. They worried there would not be enough Christians left for the church to go on, and they struggled when their children chose to marry people outside the Christian faith.

At the same time, St. James Church faced other challenges. People in general were attending worship less frequently and were less likely to join churches. This was compounded by the decline in the percentage of people coming from Christian backgrounds. How was a

Christian church to serve in a community when fewer and fewer people are Christian?

***

"Heads up. Phones down," Sara said to her teenage children as they wandered through the shopping mall. Like most other teens, Sara's son and daughter each had a smartphone, and they spent much of their lives looking down at their screens.

Sara had recently begun serving as the pastor of St. James Church. She smiled as she thought about her children and their phones, and she thought maybe she should say the same thing to the people of St. James. Not that they were always looking at their phones, but in the church it was easy to spend time looking down, looking inside the walls of the church, focusing on trying to reclaim a glorious past that was not going to return. Looking down was also a way of thinking, a way of taking care of themselves and doing little or nothing to reach out to the community.

"Heads up. Phones down." That would be a great slogan to help people remember the call for the church to be in the community as well as to care for the congregation, thought Pastor Sara. It would be a way of helping people discover ministry opportunities and needs right where they live.

In the passage from Luke at the beginning of this chapter, the lawyer was trying to get Jesus to draw lines and set limits so he could fulfill the rules and obligations as easily as possible. If Jesus had limited the definition of *neighbor* to other people like him, the lawyer would have stood a good chance of succeeding. Jesus did not do this.

In fact, the story that follows is the parable of the Good Samaritan. In this case, the hero of the story was not a faithful Jew, but a Samaritan. Faithful Jews were taught to avoid Samaritans at all costs. They were not to speak to or come into contact with them. Everyone knew Samaritans worshipped the wrong God, yet this is the hero of the story. This is the one the parable calls *neighbor*. The great shock and offense of the parable is that Jesus put no limits on the designation *neighbor*. If the Samaritan is a neighbor, then anyone and everyone is your neighbor.

Churches often have far more resources than they initially realize for serving the community. There is no promise that serving in the community suddenly fixes every budgetary concern, nor is it a guarantee that worship attendance will suddenly swell. But serving like this is a faithful response.

Grace and Glory Church, for example, had watched as the community around it changed. Many of its longtime members had moved out of the nearby neighborhood. The people who replaced them were not necessarily Christian. Joan was one of the members who stayed. One Tuesday morning, she happened to be driving by the church and for the first time noticed there was only a single car in the parking lot.

Joan thought and prayed about the future of Grace and Glory Church. She thought about the building's size, sitting there unused for much of the week. In the midst of this reflection, her phone rang. It was the president of her painting group, telling her they had lost their space to meet. Joan had just the solution: her church certainly had space.

But this was only the beginning for Joan. She started talking to others at church who belonged to various clubs and organizations. She reached out to the local Alcoholics Anonymous group. She even talked to her neighbor, who was from India, and found their Hindu congregation was looking for space for their weekly worship. Everywhere she looked, Joan discovered another group looking for inexpensive or free space for gathering. That was the easy part; convincing the congregation's leadership board was another matter. The board kept coming up with reasons to keep people out: Liability. Responsibility. Who would unlock and lock the doors? What if strangers stole or broke something? What about the added cost of electricity from lights and heating and cooling?

Joan was undaunted. She talked to other churches about how they shared their building with outside groups, then she worked with the pastor and a board member to craft building use guidelines. They identified some responsible adults in the congregation who could use a little extra income and would not mind opening and closing the building.

The second time Joan met with the congregation's leadership team, she came with a plan. First, however, she read them the parable of the Good Samaritan as a reminder that everyone around them was their neighbor. Following Jesus was about more than keeping the doors open for worship on Sunday morning.

Joan was a well-differentiated leader. She was able to handle her own anxiety and the anxiety of the group. She remained as calm as she was able to be. Her presence and low anxiety influenced Grace and Glory's leadership. They were able to listen, reflect well, and make good decisions for the church's mission and ministry.

Even more, Joan's leadership brought clarity. She reminded the board that Grace and Glory was a congregation committed to the community. One of its goals was to connect with and serve the local people, and good use of their building space was one way to reach this goal. Joan clarified for the leaders how opening the doors to others would achieve this mission goal as part of Grace and Glory's vision.

Through all this change, Joan also remained in constant contact with others. To keep folks informed, she used several different means, including email and the Grace and Glory Facebook page. This helped reduce the anxiety about this change of moving from an underused building to one that served. Folks talked with her often at worship, meetings, and other opportunities, and commended her for keeping them informed.

Within the year, the parking lot at Grace and Glory was transformed. Now the bigger challenge was managing the schedules of all the groups making use of the building. There were some added costs, but there was a new energy to the place. Occasionally, people from one of the outside groups showed up in worship, and a few of them also joined the church. Even without that, Joan was thrilled to drive by the church on a Tuesday or Wednesday morning and see the building in use.

It has been said it is easier to stop things from happening than to make them happen. Most leadership boards are gifted at keeping things the same—there is always a reason not to try something new or take a risk. Some of these concerns are valid, and the leadership is responsible for maintaining a safe and secure environment.

This is the difference between reasons and excuses. Reasons are based in reality; excuses often grow out of anxiety. Telling the Hindu group it cannot use the church's fellowship hall on Sunday mornings because the congregation is using the space for Christian education is a reason. Telling the Hindu group it cannot use the space because it might leave behind a mess and forget to properly lock the doors is an excuse. Faithful leaders will work to discern between reasons and excuses.

"Heads up, phones down" is an invitation to everyone to think creatively, dream big, and look around to discover the community's needs. Often, what starts as a simple building rental can grow into something amazing.

Grace and Glory chose to mark the first-year anniversary of the Hindu group's use of the building by sharing a meal together. At each table were people from all of the groups using the space. The food was served family style so everyone could taste a little something from another culture. The sight made Joan's heart full and brought a smile to her face.

- Where are the places your congregation has its head up? In other words, where do you see your congregation connecting with the surrounding community?

- What might it look like if people got their heads up? Where are the missed opportunities to connect with and serve your neighbors?

CHAPTER 16.

ALL LOSSES MUST BE GRIEVED

Nuclear Family Emotional System

> When Mary came where Jesus was and saw him, she knelt
> at his feet and said to him, "Lord, if you had been here, my
> brother would not have died." When Jesus saw her weeping,
> and the Jews who came with her also weeping, he was
> greatly disturbed in spirit and deeply moved. He said,
> "Where have you laid him?" They said to him, "Lord, come
> and see." Jesus began to weep. So the Jews said, "See how
> he loved him!" But some of them said, "Could not he who
> opened the eyes of the blind man have kept this man from
> dying?" (John 11:32–37)

The Bible study was about half over when Harriet found
her opening. Pastor Bill knew it was inevitable. Every
week at some point, Harriet found an excuse, however
tangential, to bring up her deceased husband. Inwardly,
Pastor Bill rolled his eyes. It wasn't that he lacked
compassion. Harriet's husband had died over twenty-five
years ago, but if you didn't know better, you would think
his funeral had been a week ago.

Plenty of people are stuck in their grief. Sometimes it
seems as if they clutch it tightly, afraid to let it go. You
can see it in the rooms at home that never change, their
closets full of clothes unworn for years after someone's

death. This is not, however, a problem reserved for individuals. Groups of people such as congregations can get stuck in grief as well.

***

The leaders at St. Thomas Church were creating a timeline of significant events in the congregation's history. Noting them on small pieces of paper, they taped the events to a long wall in chronological order. They noted when the church was founded and when its buildings were constructed. They noted significant times of growth and challenge. Then Harry reached out and taped his addition to the wall: February 2010, Pastor Jim left us.

As Jane, the leader of the event, went through the chronology, she stopped at that card. "What is this about?" she asked. "'Pastor Jim left us.' What do you mean by that?"

"Just what I wrote. That's when Pastor Jim left us," Harry said.

"But how did he leave?" Jane said. "Did he move away? Did he take another call? What?"

Susan, another member of the group, spoke up. "Pastor Jim had served here for twenty-three years, and in 2010 he retired and moved to Kansas to be near his grandchildren."

Jane smiled. "Susan, weren't you just telling us how excited you were about being retired? Don't you think Pastor Jim should have that same opportunity?"

In their heads, everyone might agree, but Harry still had a deep sense of loss and grief around his beloved pastor's retirement. He wasn't the only one. Pastor Jim had made a significant mark on the lives of the people at St. Thomas and in the surrounding community. Although people were happy for him, they still felt bereft. Many people still had emotional connections to Pastor Jim that had not been openly grieved. When there is a loss, such as Pastor Jim retiring after twenty-three years, the emotional bonds and consequent grief may remain for years. Yet, at St. Thomas, that pain and loss went unspoken. Even a decade later, the hurt was as clear as the pain Harriet carried with her every day of her life.

Everyone carries some sort of loss and grief. This is one reason why the story of the raising of Lazarus speaks so powerfully. It's not only the story of the sorrow of Mary and Martha, Lazarus's sisters; it's the story of the sorrow and grief of Jesus. In the words of the King James Version of the Bible, in all its brutal and honest simplicity, when he realized the sisters' grief at their brother's death, "Jesus wept."

This is the one we worship, the one to whom we turn in times of difficulty, suffering, and pain: the one who weeps with us. We do not travel through the darkest valleys of life alone, for Jesus goes with us.

Sometimes people discover Jesus's presence in the midst of their grief. Harold was heartbroken when his wife, June, died. They had been married for over fifty years. He had no idea how he would get along without her. It took him a couple weeks after June's funeral to go back to church.

The Sunday he finally returned, something amazing happened. Harold found himself surrounded by people who wanted to love him, and he was never alone. One couple invited him to join them afterward for lunch. The Johnsons, who always sat in the very last pew, joined him toward the front of the church. They even laughed about how they could hear and see better from the front.

The people in the congregation knew Harold's story. They knew how painful his loss was. It was as obvious as the pain of Mary and Martha at the death of their brother, Lazarus. But grief is not always so obvious.

***

Trinity Church was located in a downtown neighborhood. It had been there for nearly one hundred years. With two worship services on Sunday mornings, a modestly sized staff, and a full-time pastor, things were going well. The church had some older members who had been there for decades, and a handful of families and even a few young children making noise during worship.

Still, things were different now. There was a time when the church needed three services on Sunday mornings. There was a time when it was able to make extra mortgage payments every month. There was a time when attendance numbers always seemed to be trending up. There was a time when kids were in every grade of Sunday school and everyone knew Mrs. Franklin would be their teacher in fourth grade.

Now at Trinity Church, people sensed the world changing around them. Fewer people were walking to church because they lived further away. People who once attended three or four Sundays a month now attended only once or twice. The number of members might have looked the same on the books, but the worship numbers had decreased.

Things still looked good, but people had a sense of foreboding and a subtle anxiety. You heard it in the comments about how full the church used to be at Christmas and Easter. You heard it in mumblings about the youth group, which was down from dozens of kids to a handful.

One of Trinity Church's challenges was the unspoken grief its members were experiencing. On one level were the issues of longtime members who had died or moved away. Those realities were obvious. On another level was the grief at the loss of the church that once was. The days were gone when everything was easy.

Pastor Bill could spot glimpses of grief whenever Trinity Church made changes that suggested any sort of decline or retreat from the past. That fall, the church stopped asking youth to serve as acolytes at the early service. The reality was, more often than not, the assigned child failed to show up. With fewer than ten kids in that age group, the kids simply were not going to show up once a month. They were all too busy.

Pastor Bill had told the board he was tired of trying to hold back the ocean. If the kids weren't going to show up, for whatever reason, it made no sense to keep scheduling them for acolyte duty. A few of the older members still grumbled, "We got our kids to church at 8:00 a.m. to be acolytes. Parents these days are too soft." Pastor Bill just smiled and shook his head. The older members were right in saying the world of today is different, but he knew you cannot change that. You can only take what you can get and adapt to the realities of the day.

Beneath everyone's responses was anxiety and fear for the future. What would the church look like in five, ten, twenty years? What about when it comes time for their child's wedding or even their own funeral?

As anxiety rises, it can be increasingly difficult to think

creatively. Pastor Bill shook his head as he listened to the other ideas his leadership board proposed at their meeting. Sally thought the best way to get people to the church was to send out large, full-color postcards to the ten thousand homes around the church. "Even if only a few people respond, it could easily be more than worth it," she argued. Marquis was in favor of robo-calling—he had seen an ad for a company that could call every cell phone in the community for a small price. Lance wanted to buy a huge digital sign—he said the sign company assured him the $30,000 sign would pay for itself in just a few years.

In addition to finding it hard to think creatively, when anxiety rises, it becomes more difficult for people to hear what others are saying in the situation. Pastor Bill may have been spotting inevitable changes, such as the acolytes at the early service, but the leaders were so anxious that they didn't really hear him; they didn't acknowledge the reality they were facing.

Anxiety robs us of our creativity and ability to listen well, but it also makes it difficult for us to learn. Trinity Church's leadership may have benefitted from attending a workshop at which they could learn that focusing on the congregation's strengths can help reduce the anxiety behind their lack of creative thinking, lessen the emotional deafness hampering their ability to hear one another, and stop preventing possible learning opportunities.

But the Trinity Church board couldn't get past its anxieties. So once again all it did was make minor repairs and quick fixes to the church's congregational life, because the board members thought there was nothing wrong with the way they had been doing things. All their programming was first-class, or at least good enough, they thought. Their building was welcoming and in good repair. Their sanctuary was beautiful. All they needed to do was advertise and give the youth program a little boost. That would fix everything.

Every time there is another reduction, every time there is another decision that seems like a step backward, the unspoken grief increases. Seeing this, Pastor Bill made plans to name this difficult reality at the next board meeting. He decided it was time to be honest about the truth of the congregation. The time for making bold choices and taking risks in doing things in new and different ways was now, while the congregation was still strong and viable. The church needed to consider its congregation's strengths and how it could enhance its mission by using those strengths to move into a new future. He hoped that by naming the congregation's fears and anxieties and grief, it would help people own that and move forward for the sake of the gospel.

- What are the unspoken griefs in the life of your congregation?
- How does anxiety and worry keep your congregation from trying new things for the sake of the gospel?

CHAPTER 17.

HELP ME FIX HIM!

Triangling

Now he was teaching in one of the synagogues on the Sabbath. And just then there appeared a woman with a spirit that had crippled her for eighteen years. She was bent over and was quite unable to stand up straight. When Jesus saw her, he called her over and said, "Woman, you are set free from your ailment." When he laid his hands on her, immediately she stood up straight and began praising God. But the leader of the synagogue, indignant because Jesus had cured on the Sabbath, kept saying to the crowd, "There are six days on which work ought to be done; come on those days and be cured, and not on the Sabbath day." But the Lord answered him and said, "You hypocrites! Does not each of you on the Sabbath untie his ox or his donkey from the manger and lead it away to give it water? And ought not this woman, a daughter of Abraham whom Satan bound for eighteen long years, be set free from this bondage on the Sabbath day?" When he said this, all his opponents were put to shame, and the entire crowd was rejoicing at all the wonderful things that he was doing. (Luke 13:10–17)

John and his fourteen-year-old son, Jared, arrived about an hour early for Jared's basketball game. This meant Jared would have plenty of time to warm up and John could watch the younger team in their club—the

Springfield Slammers—play. There were four different games going on in the same huge gym. The sound of basketballs, whistles, and coaches yelling echoed throughout the space.

Even with all the chaos, one voice rose above the rest. That voice belonged to the coach of the team opposing the Slammers. From what the coach was saying, this was the most incompetently officiated game in the history of basketball. Apparently, the referee was lousy. The Slammers were allegedly playing a dirty and vicious version of basketball—although to John's eyes it looked like every other game he had ever witnessed.

As John watched, he noticed one other curious thing: every time the coach yelled at the referee, he followed up by turning to the parents in the stands behind him and yelling, "Can you believe this ref? The Slammers are a dirty team, I tell you." His derogatory comments were almost incessant. Even when a call went in his favor, it was not enough. This coach was way too invested in the outcome of a game played by a bunch of twelve-year-old boys.

Early in the second half, everything fell apart. John was standing near the court, watching the game, when he heard a roar. He turned to see parents from both teams throwing punches at each other in the stands. That was the end for the parents and for the kids—the referees canceled the rest of the game. The fighters were pulled apart. Children were scared and crying. Within ten minutes, police officers were wandering through the gym to keep the peace.

John pulled his son away from the swarm and they went outside to wait for things to calm down. Reflecting on what had happened, John became convinced the other team's coach was highly anxious. John wasn't even sure the anxiety had anything to do with the basketball game. But the coach had taken out his anxiety on the referee, and when the referee refused to deal with him, he turned to the parents to get them on his side. That was the choice that pushed everything over the edge. By his logic, parents who deeply loved their children and wanted them to succeed needed to recognize the one thing holding their children back: allegedly, the other team's dirty play and the referee's poor work.

This is a classic example of triangling. Triangling occurs when two people cannot deal with the anxiety between them, so they enlist a third person to be on their side and support them over the other. The coach could not deal with his feelings about the game. He took them out on the referee, but this only lasted so long. Eventually, the referee called technical fouls on the coach. The coach drew in a third person—in this case, his team's supportive parents. They were more than willing to accept his anxiety . . . until it boiled over into a fistfight in the stands.

We see this dynamic at play in the gospel as well. Jesus had done the unthinkable: he healed on the Sabbath. Faithful Jews knew you do not work on the Sabbath. This was not just some arbitrary rule, but a fundamental aspect of their identity as people of faith. The synagogue leader was angry with Jesus, but he could not bring himself to speak to him directly. Instead, he turned to the crowd and complained to them, hoping to get them on his side and take care of this upstart, Jesus. The problem with this choice is that it rarely moves the conversation forward toward a resolution.

Jesus, however, was interested in moving the conversation forward. Rather than trying to compete with the synagogue's leader for the crowd's attention, Jesus addressed the crowd directly. Jesus reminded them of his calling to free people from bondage. This was exactly why he did not hesitate to heal a woman who had been suffering and bent over for the last eighteen years. Jesus connected directly with the people who were challenging him and reminded them of his mission in the world.

***

Gordon and his wife, Kim, had just returned to worship at Good Shepherd Church after spending their winter down in Florida. When he opened the bulletin on his first Sunday back, Gordon was confused. Instead of the usual three scripture readings, there was just one long reading from some Old Testament book. Nothing from St. Paul. Nothing from the gospels. What was going on?

Pastor Sam had been serving at Good Shepherd for a couple years and things had stayed pretty much the same—until this nonsense. Gordon figured talking directly with Pastor Sam would be a waste of time, so he decided instead to go right to the board president, Judy, and get her to deal with the pastor. This could not go on!

On the phone with Judy, Gordon was adamant. He expected to see the three usual readings back in worship the next Sunday—or else! Judy tried to explain the idea behind the Narrative Lectionary. She described it as a yearlong experiment, allowing the congregation to dig deeper into often overlooked books of the Bible.

Gordon continued ranting as if he had not heard a thing Judy said. Then she realized this wasn't her fight. Gordon was angry with the changes led by Pastor Sam—if anything was to be done, Gordon would need to talk to him. "Gordon, I can tell this is really bothering you," Judy said. "Using the Narrative Lectionary was Pastor Sam's idea. It seems you need to speak directly with him about your concerns."

Judy was trying to remove herself from the triangle formed between herself and Gordon and Pastor Sam. If anything was to change, Gordon and the pastor needed to talk directly. Gordon said he would think about it, but left things at that.

Gordon and Kim kept going to worship, but he spent most of the worship service with his arms crossed. His face looked like he had eaten lemon slices for breakfast.

Then one Saturday afternoon, Gordon missed a step and fell as he was walking out of the house. He tried to get up, but he could not move his right leg at all. His hip was broken. As he was being wheeled into the emergency room, he looked up and saw Pastor Sam standing in the hallway. Even though it was a Saturday afternoon, his pastor had dropped everything and come to the hospital to pray for him.

Gordon was still in pain as he waited for the tests to confirm everything they already knew. He looked up at Pastor Sam. "Thanks for coming," he said. "You know I have not been thrilled about some of the changes you made while we were down south. I know you have been trying to talk to me, but I was avoiding you. Now here you are, praying for me."

"I knew something was up," Pastor Sam said, "but I wasn't sure what it was. I would be glad to talk with you after you get your hip fixed."

Gordon smiled. "Yes, the hip is a priority! Lying here,

worrying about recovering, the readings in worship don't seem to matter that much."

Pastor Sam reflected on their conversation as he drove home for dinner. He had sensed something was off with Gordon but figured giving Gordon time to process it was his best move. When he got home, he called Juanita, who was in charge of the church meal train. They would make sure Gordon and Kim had some home-cooked meals when Gordon got home from the hospital.

Judy was glad to hear Gordon and Pastor Sam had finally had a chance to talk things through. She was sad it had taken so long, but that is the way it is sometimes. She knew a triangle is never a good way to move a conversation toward resolution. She also knew Gordon tended to get upset over small things every so often, and he tended to try to find someone else to fix those things for him. Judy knew that far more important was the relationship between Gordon and Pastor Sam. If Gordon was always mad and distant from the pastor, whoever that was, how could he hear the good news of Jesus? Judy knew this wouldn't be the last time this sort of thing could happen, but at least she felt prepared to leave the anxiety where it belonged: with Gordon. *We really have to talk to one another*, Judy thought, *not about one another!*

- Where can you find triangular relationships in your congregation?
- When have you found yourself giving your anxiety to another person?

CHAPTER 18.

THIS IS SERVING IN CHRIST'S NAME

Self-Differentiation

> But you are a chosen race, a royal priesthood, a holy nation, God's own people, in order that you may proclaim the mighty acts of him who called you out of darkness into his marvelous light. Once you were not a people, but now you are God's people; once you had not received mercy, but now you have received mercy. (1 Pet 2:9–10)

Isn't this what it's all about? Ken asked himself at the dedication of the newly built Faith House. *Yes, this is serving in Christ's name!* he thought.

Ken had joined others over the past few months to build this new home for Yolanda and her three children. It was called the Faith House. Three other congregations joined Madison Road Evangelical Church (MRE) in doing the work. Yolanda had done much of the work with them, spending countless hours at the project site. Even her eldest son, twelve-year-old Elroy, pitched in to help.

It meant so much to Yolanda and her family to have their own home. Today was the celebration service at which the keys would be given to Yolanda. This new place, this new home, was now hers to share with her family. *Yes, this is what it's all about*, Ken thought.

For Ken and the people of MRE, this was the end of the story, while Yolanda and her family's story was only just beginning. Still, beginnings and endings can be tricky. For some people, the story began when the building permit was obtained, financing was arranged, and the actual work commenced. Others would say the story began long before the first shovel sliced into the dirt to dig the foundation.

In the end, it is not even a story of building a house at all. It is a story about relationships and how leaders who are well self-differentiated can contribute to a healthy system, making serving in Christ's name possible. Let's trace the roots of the process and see how such leadership made this new home a reality for Yolanda and her family.

The process began early in January, when Pastor Megan encouraged MRE's board members to attend a daylong retreat with a special consultant, Michelle. Michelle was coming to help the leaders define why MRE was a congregation and to set a vision for the year.

Michelle began promptly at 9:00 a.m. Over the course of the morning, all twelve of the board members learned how their congregation was like a family system with all kinds of relationships influencing others within it so ministry and mission could be accomplished. Through an enjoyable process, Michelle led the leaders in identifying and writing their congregation's mission statement. She had them draw what they saw was the purpose of MRE. At first, people were reluctant to display their lack of artistic ability, but after some good-hearted cajoling, they saw the point of the exercise. By using images, even poorly drawn stick figures, the conversation shifted from perfect words to images of their life together as a congregation. Eventually, their result was this statement: "Loved by God, serving."

This met all the requirements for a good mission statement. It was one sentence long, simple enough for a twelve-year-old to understand, and easily memorized. The process took a while, but the leaders were pleased with the result. "Loved by God, serving" became the umbrella under which they would make important decisions in the coming years. The retreat was productive.

In addition to the mission statement, Michelle led the leaders in articulating three important goals for the year. What would they focus on as a congregation for this calendar year? What was their immediate vision for MRE? They had revealed their why—"Loved by God, serving." Now it was their opportunity as the royal priesthood called by God to decide how they would live out their mission as a gathered community serving in Christ's name.

A couple board members had a long list of potential ministry opportunities. Michelle explained how difficult it is for congregations to handle more than three goals in a year. Most churches can do only one or two well. With too many choices, nothing gets done.

The board worked hard through another process led by Michelle, trimming down the year's vision and goals. The members ultimately decided on two as their focus: participating with the three other congregations in the Faith House and strengthening their education programs for faith formation. One goal looked outward and served the community, and the other looked inward and served MRE. They thought this was a good balance and ministry they could achieve. The MRE leadership had moved from a haphazard approach of being a church to a more focused ministry, which would allow them to serve in Christ's name as the royal priesthood. It was a good day for the leaders.

It wasn't long after the retreat that Aaron, the board president, asked Ken if he had a moment to chat. In a conversation in the library at church, Aaron asked if Ken would chair a committee to make it possible for MRE to participate in the Faith House for Yolanda and her family. There would be three parts to Ken's leadership. The first priority was recruiting folks to do the actual work on the house. The second was to enlist a lunch group to prepare and serve the daily meal for the workers. The third priority would be for Ken to make a series of inspiring speeches to help raise the $10,000 required as their church's share of the construction costs.

"Take a week to consider this prayerfully," Aaron suggested. If Ken said yes, it would be a big undertaking and lots of responsibility. Ken said he would think it over.

Next Sunday in church, Ken pulled Aaron aside. "I'm saying yes about chairing the Faith House committee," Ken said. "I will do it."

"This is great," Aaron said. "Let's get together on Tuesday to talk about specifics and the people you may want to recruit."

At their Tuesday meeting, over coffee, they decided three subcommittees were needed. The first would be workers. They agreed that Bruce, with his architectural and building background, would be ideal for recruiting and supervising the actual workers. Forming and leading the lunch group might be Mustafa. He had lots of experience feeding groups as a volunteer at the homeless shelter in town. Finally, Ken said he would head the generosity committee, as he called it, to seek the offerings that would produce the $10,000 needed. Aaron double-checked with Ken about this, worried it might be too much, but Ken explained he felt a definite call to head up the generosity committee. Aaron approved.

Ken felt blessed by God for all the marvelous gifts he had been given. He felt blessed even when Missy, his wife, died young from breast cancer and he was left to raise their ten-year-old twins alone. Brit, their daughter, was now married and happy in her new job. Rick, their son, had one more year of college, then he would be out and on his own. He was looking forward to being the electrical engineer he was studying hard to be. Yes, Ken felt blessed. "God is good," he always said. Living in the grace of God, in the forgiveness of the cross, Ken felt, he could commit time, energy, and even money to such a good ministry as the Faith House.

Both Bruce and Mustafa said yes when Ken asked them to serve in their roles. Ken had told them MRE's new mission statement was "Loved by God, serving" and the church's vision for this year had two projects, one being the Faith House. Bruce and Mustafa saw the focus and the goals and immediately signed on to help reach them.

Over the months of building the house for Yolanda and her family, Bruce and Mustafa faithfully led their committees. When it was time for MRE to work on the build, Bruce had assembled a good, hardworking crew. In fact, one Saturday, Bruce had enough workers that he was needed only to supervise.

Mustafa also found people more than willing to help with meals. Like Ken had done for him, Mustafa shared the church's mission statement and the vision for the year, and people saw how they could fit in and serve as the royal priesthood. Yes, there was one Saturday when Mustafa had to scramble a bit to get things together, but with a couple pizzas added to what people had made, all was well.

Raising the funds was a challenge Ken had undertaken, one he felt called to do. The first thing he did was ask Marisol to work with him. Marisol was a good writer and speaker, and she was more than willing to help. When Ken explained the focus under "Loved by God, serving" was to participate in the Faith House, Marisol signed on immediately.

Ken and Marisol decided they would focus people on gratitude and giving. Marisol pointed out how loved and forgiven we are by God. Living in the shadow of the cross, she said, we are a people of grace who are grateful. From this foundation of gratitude for all we are and have as gifts from God, Marisol worked up a process to encourage people to contribute to the Faith House fund.

Over several months, they held cottage meetings in homes, supplied people with weekly updates about the build, wrote a letter to the entire congregation explaining the ministry, and invited folks to make special gifts over and above their regular support of the congregation. They even provided special envelopes for the cause.

It was a great joy when they reached and then far surpassed the $10,000 challenge. Ken and Marisol thanked the congregation for their faithfulness. They thanked them also for their gratitude, which acknowledged how God had blessed them all so they could be a blessing for others as they served in the royal priesthood by making their contributions.

Fred, an older member of the parish, was especially delighted to give a substantial gift. "I am too old and not able to swing a hammer anymore," he told Ken, "but I am pleased we are doing this Faith House and I want to support it. It has been a long time since Madison Road Evangelical did actual hands-on ministry in our community. I am happy to make a special monetary contribution."

You can see why Ken was saying to himself at the home's dedication and the passing of the keys to Yolanda, *For us*, this *is what it's all about*. Ken had learned that MRE was like a large family system. How the leaders functioned made a difference in how everyone else acted. It began with the board being willing to spend the time to answer the why question and then the how question. Why? "Loved by God, serving." How? Through a vision of ministry in the community and in the congregation: the Faith House and the emphasis on educating for faith formation.

With this clear vision, the work of recruiting folks became much easier. Leaders, including Aaron and Ken, were able to recruit key people by remaining calm, being clear, and staying connected to the folks. Well-defined, thoughtful leadership that focused on self set the tone, and this allowed others to serve well. It may seem odd to focus on self, but if we fail to regulate our own anxiety and remain calm, define ourselves clearly, and connect to others, our impact as leaders on the system may be unhealthy. Thus, we focus on self not in an egotistical way, but as leaders who know being clear, calm, and connected encourages healthier leading.

When there were bumps along the way and anxiety arose in the group, Aaron and Ken's calm, clear, and connected leadership made it possible to assess the situation carefully, reflect on what to do, and confidently choose a path ahead.

This leadership of calm, clear, and connected folks was also key to the generosity campaign. As you would expect, when Marisol and Ken introduced the fund drive and placed before the congregation the $10,000 goal, Herman was immediately a critic. He stood at the first meeting and complained about how hard it was just to keep things afloat at MRE. How could the church be spending more, he asked, when it was so difficult to do what it was doing now? "This is too much," he said. "It's impossible to do and we aren't even spending it on ourselves."

Charles stood up in the meeting and countered Herman. "Remember Mr. Rodney Green? He always said, 'Madison Road Evangelical accomplishes whatever goal it sets before itself,'" Charles said. "Now, I agree with Mr. Green. I have been a member of MRE all my life and I cannot remember ever failing to meet a challenge when we worked together. I am confident we can meet this challenge just as we have met so many in the past." With that, the congregation voted to meet the $10,000 goal. Folks came up to Ken and Marisol afterward and personally pledged they would be giving to the Faith House fund.

This was calm, clear, connected leadership that responded rather than reacted when anxiety rose in the congregation. Herman did his best to spread his anxiety at the meeting, but Charles brought a calm, clear, connected perspective that reduced the anxiety. All this was possible because the leadership had spent the time and energy to write a mission statement, discern a vision, then invite the congregation to join them in serving as the royal priesthood.

Did you notice the relationship results? If you count the leaders and others mentioned in this story, you will find there were lots of folks. Pastor Megan, Ken, Aaron, Bruce, Mustafa, Marisol, Fred, Yolanda, Charles, and more were part of this ministry, together building a home for a family that needed one. Like ripples from a stone dropped in a lake, all these people touched others as they served. All kinds of relationships were created, sustained, and strengthened as the Faith House proceeded. Present and well-functioning leadership makes a difference for so many relationships and encourages more service in Christ's name.

- When has your congregation answered the why and how questions?

- As a leader, how do you focus on yourself so you remain calm, clear, and connected when anxiety rises in your congregation?

CHAPTER 19.

HEY, THAT'S MY TRIGGER!

Nuclear Family Emotional System

Then they seized him and led him away, bringing him into the high priest's house. But Peter was following at a distance. When they had kindled a fire in the middle of the courtyard and sat down together, Peter sat among them. Then a servant girl, seeing him in the firelight, stared at him and said, "This man also was with him." But he denied it, saying, "Woman, I do not know him." A little later someone else, on seeing him, said, "You also are one of them." But Peter said, "Man, I am not!" Then about an hour later still another kept insisting, "Surely this man also was with him, for he is a Galilean." But Peter said, "Man, I do not know what you are talking about!" At that moment, while he was still speaking, the cock crowed. The Lord turned and looked at Peter. Then Peter remembered the word of the Lord, how he had said to him, "Before the cock crows today, you will deny me three times." And he went out and wept bitterly. (Luke 22:54–62)

Joe sighed. He had been a member of the worship committee at St. James Church for only two months and he already hated the job. Well, that wasn't entirely true. He loved the committee work. He liked getting together with the others and talking about the coming months of worship and the seasons of the church year. He felt as if he was getting a feel for the flow of the church year for the first time in his life. The work itself was not the problem. The problem was Daniel's "stuckness."

On a Sunday morning in early October, Joe and his wife, Linda, were just about to head into church when Joe saw Daniel coming at him with a full head of steam. Joe rolled his eyes. He didn't need Daniel to say a single word. Joe knew exactly what was coming, and once again, Daniel did not disappoint.

"Hey, Joe," Daniel said, "are we gonna be praying about our sins again, or has the worship committee finally come to its senses and let us have trespasses back?"

There it was. Daniel despised the newer translation of the Lord's Prayer St. James Church had been using in worship for the last month. Daniel knew Joe was the newest member of the worship committee and he pegged him as a weak link. Daniel seemed to think if he could get Joe on his side, the worship committee would never change the Lord's Prayer again, and that would be just fine with Daniel.

Joe felt trapped. He wanted to be able to worship in peace. He wanted Sunday morning to be a time when he could forget about all the stuff of the past week, let everything go, and connect with God. Daniel was making that impossible—this was the third Sunday in a row he had brought this up. Joe snapped. "Daniel," he said. "I am sick and tired of listening to you complain about the different translation of the Lord's Prayer. At this point, even if I agreed with you—which I don't—I would be against you, because you are so annoying."

With that, Joe snatched a bulletin out of the usher's hand and stomped into church, his wife trailing behind. Daniel stood for a second with his mouth hanging open, then he harrumphed, grabbed a bulletin, and found a seat as far away from Joe as possible.

We all have our breaking points, those times when we just do not want to hear it one more time. When we do, we are triggered. We lash out, saying things we sometimes regret later. We trample on other people's feelings. There might have been a good reason that particular translation of the Lord's Prayer was so important to Daniel, but Joe would never find out because he was too frustrated and angry.

This is what happens when we are triggered. Our thoughtful and reflective brain stops working and the reptilian brain—which fights, freezes, or pushes us to flee—takes over. This is the reactive part of our brain. It can be useful at times. When the car in front of you suddenly slams on the brakes, you don't even have to think. You simply react, moving your right foot from the gas to the brake and pushing down hard. This reaction is good. It keeps us safe.

When the threat is not a car crash but a repeated annoying behavior, this is a completely different situation. Now it is about relationships, and maintaining healthy ones often requires a more nuanced and subtle approach.

One of the gifts of being in a community for a longer period of time is that you get to know people. After a few weeks, Joe knew exactly what was coming from Daniel. He said so himself. That being the case, why bother to get angry?

Everyone has people in their lives who trigger them. Everyone reacts at one time or another. But if you know it is coming, you have an advantage. You can plan your responses ahead of time. You can think through your feelings. Then, when the moment comes, you're prepared.

A couple weeks later, Joe saw Daniel at church and this time chose not to avoid him. Instead, he sought Daniel out. "Daniel," Joe said, "I am sorry for the way I reacted to you a while ago. I was frustrated because every single Sunday you complained to me about the Lord's Prayer. It got to the point that I was dreading coming to church."

"Well, it really bothers me," Daniel said. "That's the prayer I've known since I was a little boy, and it feels like it was stolen from me."

"I hear you," Joe said, "but here's what I need you to know: The worship committee has already heard your complaint. It will certainly be discussed, but I cannot promise any changes. I can tell you I have heard you, so we will not have this conversation again. I refuse to allow you to ruin my Sunday mornings."

Daniel tried to bring it up one more time the following Sunday, but Joe simply said, "Good morning" and walked on by to the coffee pot. Joe wasn't entirely comfortable with his handling of the situation, but Sunday mornings sure felt better. He even worked with Daniel a few weeks later, setting up tables and chairs for a fellowship event.

When everything was done, Daniel smiled at Joe and shook his hand. "I have to tell you, Joe," Daniel said, "at first when you stopped listening to me complain, I was annoyed. But you were right. It wasn't fair of me to attack you every Sunday. That's not the right way to go about things. I know *I* need an hour of peace for worship and I am sure you do too. This new prayer still bugs me, but I guess I'll just have to deal with it myself."

"Thanks, Daniel," Joe said. "I appreciate that. And I have

some good news for you. Starting in Lent, we'll be back to the prayer you like."

***

The account of Peter denying Jesus three times as Jesus faced the cross and death is the story of a man being triggered. In his case, self-preservation triggered the denials. Peter was reacting to folks recognizing him as a disciple of Jesus. He saw things were not going well and he wanted to defend himself against the crowd, which wanted to align him with Jesus. He was worried that, like Jesus, he would be seized and tried by the Romans. He was thinking with his reptilian or lower brain, which made him defensive. Peter was doing whatever he could to save himself, because he literally feared for his life.

You can't really blame Peter for being so anxious and reactive. It was a dismal time, and the anxiety was intense in the moment. So, he reverted to the primitive reaction of the reptilian brain and distanced himself from Jesus. Peter's trigger was what he perceived to be a threat to his life. There's little wonder why he was so reactive, rather than being thoughtful about his situation.

***

Is there a way for a board member to be thoughtful rather than reactive when a trigger makes them want to live in the reptilian part of the brain? Let's listen to Susan in this example.

Susan was her congregation's board president. After a conference she attended for work, she saw some similar patterns in the church board. A couple people seemed to have the same issues meeting after meeting. No matter what changes were made, no matter the topic, they managed to drag the discussion back to their issue at virtually every meeting.

Susan was glad to identify this. She had learned that identifying the problem was a great first step. Next, the conference facilitator had suggested pretending to watch yourself in the conversation, as if on TV or through a one-way mirror. This way, you could be a more detached observer.

At the next meeting, Susan tried this. She found that when she watched from a distance, she was less emotional and reactive. She was able to hear the other person and formulate appropriate responses. In this situation, Susan chose to redirect the conversation to the topic at hand and not to the pet topic of the member in question. The member did not seem thrilled by this change, but the board was able to have a productive discussion and make good, thoughtful decisions.

- What if Peter had been more of an observer from a distance? Might his response to those who accused him be different than denying Jesus?

- Can you think of alternate responses if Peter had observed the situation from a distance?

- What are your triggers?

- How have you tried to manage your reactions? Can you watch from a distance? Think of some examples of when you managed to do this and when you didn't. What were the outcomes?

CHAPTER 20.

WHO CAN WE BLAME?

Family Projection

> As [Jesus] walked along, he saw a man blind from birth. His disciples asked him, "Rabbi, who sinned, this man or his parents, that he was born blind?" Jesus answered, "Neither this man nor his parents sinned; he was born blind so that God's works might be revealed in him." (John 9:1–3)

Who is to blame for the man born blind? It must be someone's fault, right? Anytime something goes wrong, it is common to place blame, find a scapegoat—and make sure the fingers aren't pointing at you.

John was diagnosed with lung cancer. Incredulous, he said to the doctor, "I have never smoked a single cigarette, not even a secret puff as a kid. How could this happen to me?"

He was tempted to blame his parents for the secondhand smoke he had breathed as a child, because, like many people in their generation, they were smokers. Of course, by the time John was diagnosed, they had been dead for years.

After John died from his cancer, his family went out of their way at his memorial service to make sure everyone knew John was among the small percentage of people who developed lung cancer despite never having smoked. They did not want people to blame John for the cancer. No one wants to end up being blamed when bad things happen.

***

St. Luke Church was located just a couple miles from a large graduated care facility, one of those places with everything from assisted living to memory care. For some time, people in the facility's assisted living portion drove to St. Luke every Sunday.

Recently, the pastor learned some of those folks had stopped driving, which meant they had stopped going to church. At the annual budget meeting, the congregation voted to fund the purchase of a van to pick up people from the facility and drive them back and forth to church. Members were energized and excited to begin this new ministry.

At the next board meeting, Kyan volunteered to take on the job of finding the right van. After budgeting for insurance and maintenance, there was only enough money for a used van, but Kyan had a friend who was selling one that would be perfect. With a handshake and a smile Kyan sealed the deal, and by the next week the new van was in the church's parking.

For the first few weeks, everything went smoothly and there were ten people from the care facility in worship. The next week, it rained—a huge downpour. The van was at a stop sign almost exactly halfway to the church when it stalled and refused to start. The driver made some calls, and as the van was towed to a repair shop, a caravan of cars and SUVs left the church to pick up the stranded people.

The repair shop said the issue was something about valves, spark plugs, and a few other things. In the end, the bill came to nearly $1,000. People were not happy with Kyan, and they were even less happy when the van stalled out again the next week, this time on the return trip. The repeat problem made it difficult to round up volunteer drivers a second time.

At the next board meeting, Kyan was in the hot seat, faced with a barrage of questions and barbed comments: "Just where did you find this van, the junk yard?" "How much more are we going to have to spend?" "If this happens in the middle of winter, people could freeze to death!"

Kyan was having none of it. "You didn't authorize enough money to get something new and in excellent shape, and I had the van towed to the mechanic George suggested." George was the board president, who was looking a bit anxious himself.

"Well, I don't know anything about cars, but even I can tell those tires are almost bald," Valarie said.

"Those tires are just fine—they'll get us through the winter. Tires routinely need to be replaced," Kyan said. "I should have known better than to trust that friend of mine. He never maintains anything. We should call him and get our money back."

"Maybe this whole thing isn't worth the bother," Kendra said. "I bet those people from the old folks' home don't give much money anyway. This is going to cost us nothing but money, no matter what we do."

The meeting ended without a decision about how to move forward. The next Sunday, the van sat in the parking lot and the people in the care facility stayed put. Kyan stayed home that day as well. The last thing he wanted was to show up at church and be reminded of his role in the debacle.

When things go wrong, it is tempting to find someone else to blame. No one wants to be the one everyone considers to be responsible for the failure. The trouble is that blame does not move toward solutions to issues. In the blame game, it is easy for a group to find themselves stuck and feeling hopeless.

But when individuals in the group take responsibility for their own emotions, things can progress. When time is allowed for decisions to be made carefully, then it is more common for the group to share responsibility. Taking time to assess the situation and reflect on it carefully and patiently will lead to a confident action by the board. Assessing, reflecting, and moving ahead confidently all help avoid needless blaming.

If the board had moved more deliberately, things might have turned out differently. What if it had sent Kyan out to find the true costs of the possible choices before the congregational meeting? If more people had known they were short of the funds necessary to buy a more reliable vehicle, maybe the money could have been found before the board made the purchase. Kyan could also have made clear the risks involved in purchasing the used vehicle. Sharing this with the board before the purchase would have made the choice a shared one rather than his alone.

What about the board's understanding of the church's ministry? In a contentious meeting, someone needs to be willing to remind the group of its purpose. What if someone had said, "I am disappointed and frustrated by the situation with the van, but we have to accept where we are and move on. We agreed part of our calling is to share the good news of Jesus with others, so how are we going to share the gospel with the people at the retirement home?" If no one works to shift the conversation, ministry will soon grind to a halt. Fewer and fewer people will volunteer for leadership roles fearing that any failure, real or perceived, will be blamed on them.

Things will go wrong from time to time. The church is filled with humans who do not always get things right. The challenge is not to avoid mistakes but to respond calmly and creatively when they do. By carefully assessing the ministry challenge, reflecting on it, and then creating a plan that can be carried out confidently, decision-making will be healthier and will move the congregation ahead to reach its goals.

***

This can also apply to what we do as individuals in challenging situations. A few months ago, Pastor Bill's longtime friend and neighbor Jim invited him to come to his parent's fiftieth wedding anniversary party and to preside at their renewal of vows. Jim was planning it as a surprise.

"I've known your parents for a few years," Pastor Bill said, "and I know them to be strong Roman Catholics. Are you sure a Lutheran pastor like me is the right one for the job?"

"They love you, Bill. Don't worry, they will really appreciate it," Jim said.

After a bit of this back and forth, Pastor Bill relented and put the event in his calendar. When the big day came,

Pastor Bill arrived at the restaurant with a nicely printed renewal of marriage vows ceremony in hand. As he walked into the room filled with fifty or sixty people, Jim greeted Pastor Bill with a smile, patted him on the back, and guided him into the room.

"Hey, everyone, it's time for the big surprise! Pastor Bill is here so Mom and Dad can renew their marriage vows," Jim announced.

Jim's mother stood up with a look of horror on her face. It was clear she did not want a Lutheran pastor to lead her through renewing her Roman Catholic marriage vows. She glanced at her husband, then looked to her right and smiled. "Father Timothy, you are the one who married us fifty years ago. How about you do the renewal ceremony," she said.

After some quick negotiations, it was agreed Pastor Bill would read a passage of scripture, then Father Timothy would take over and lead the rest of the service. The priest even added a Catholic version of the final blessing.

Pastor Bill smiled to himself through it all. When the ceremony was over, he stood up, clinked his glass with a spoon, and said, "Isn't it time to kiss the bride?"

Pastor Bill certainly felt insulted, but he was not surprised by the events. In fact, he half expected something like this to happen. Rather than be angry and blame Jim or Jim's parents, he chose to make the best of a bad situation and laugh at the craziness of it all. Pastor Bill smiled when he thought about how Jim seemed to have no idea that his parents would not want a Lutheran leading the service. Pastor Bill declined the invitation to stay for lunch, claiming another engagement.

Pastor Bill wasn't angry because he saw the afternoon as a study in family systems theory. He learned much about Jim, his parents, and their life of faith. He saw the connection between the couple renewing their vows and Father Timothy. He saw the connection between Jim, his parents, and the faith in which Jim had been raised and which he now lived out.

Pastor Bill understood his role in it all. He knew reacting and acting offended would only have ruined a wonderful celebration for Jim's parents—which was the last thing he wanted to do. Viewed from a larger perspective, Pastor Bill was able to make the best of an uncomfortable situation and still had time to meet his wife for a late lunch. He took a moment to assess the situation, reflected on how it could best be addressed, and moved ahead confidently, reading scripture and joining in the celebration.

It is easy to fall into the pit of blame. Blame also lets people off the hook. If you blame someone or something else, you don't have to take responsibility for your role in a bad situation. You don't have to worry about making things better. After all, it's not your fault.

The way out becomes clear by looking at the larger picture. For Pastor Bill, it meant wanting Jim's parents to have a special day they could remember fondly. In the case of St. Luke Church, it meant focusing on its calling to share the good news of Jesus with people who were unable to drive themselves to church.

In every ministry, things will go poorly once in a while. An event for which many people labored faithfully will be sparsely attended, or there will be mistakes, misprints, and typos in printed and published materials. There will be failures. That is inevitable. The question is not how to make sure we will avoid mistakes, but how to focus on our vision for mission when things go wrong.

- Can you remember a time you played the blame game? Describe the experience.

- When was a time someone pointed you back to the big-picture vision for your ministry?

EPILOGUE

It was a warm June evening when Zion Church's leadership board gathered at Moshe's home for its meeting and end-of-year cookout. Moshe was completing his year as board president, so he chose to start the evening with a toast.

"Raise your iced tea with me," Moshe announced. "Here's to a great year. We faced challenges together and remained focused on moving forward, and Zion Church has thrived because of your efforts!"

Board members clinked glasses around the table as they recalled the past year. Things had not started out smoothly. The preschool director had resigned and hinted she was forced out, and there had been some drama over the preferred translation of the Lord's Prayer used in worship, along with the usual stresses and strains of congregational life.

Glenys tapped the side of her glass and everyone quieted down. "I must say," Glenys began, "I was a little dismayed when the preschool director quit suddenly. She was so good for so long, and I wasn't sure what would happen next. Then we made a plan, began interviewing people, and worked through a process. The more we focused on the process, the less the minor complaints mattered. Now we have an excellent replacement, one I hope will serve for many years. To process!"

Seamus spoke up next. "When some people emailed me and said I just didn't care about them or their feelings, at first I got mad. I wanted to give them a piece of my mind. But then I took a deep breath and calmed down. I could literally feel my heart rate slow. Once I did that, I saw those folks were only speaking out of their own pain, which might have had less to do with the specific changes we had made than with something in their lives. Focusing on myself really made a difference." Seamus paused and smiled. "The toast 'Here's to me' doesn't sound quite right, but it's all I have. Cheers!"

"I had been so tired of all the negativity," Manisha said next, "everyone talking about what we cannot do. I am so glad we spent the year focusing on what we *can* do with our strengths. We have way more resources than we imagined!"

"I am relieved we do not all have to agree about everything all the time. Trying for perfect unity was exhausting," Ramirez said. "I appreciate being able to be a person of integrity and have a position, even when we do not all agree. As they say in Norway, *skol!*"

"Keeping everyone happy and comfortable all the time has gotten us nowhere," Aaliyah agreed. "My heart was full this year when I watched people rise to the challenges we placed before them."

Xander raised his iced tea glass, now only half full. "Looks like we have just enough for a couple more toasts," he said, "so here's to looking at the church as an interconnected system and not just separate parts. This made so much sense to me when we started seeing all the connections between people and groups. *Salud!*"

"I guess it is my turn now," Isla said, "so here's to knowing where we are going and focusing on our direction, not the day-to-day conditions of everything. That has made a huge difference. Cheers!"

"As the host, I claim the last toast," Moshe said, surveying the table of smiling faces. "When I started as board president, I was nervous. There was so much worry and anxiety in the church. We still have huge challenges, and the world is certainly different than it was forty years ago, but I feel different now. I am confident we can rise to the occasion, look to the future with hope, and manage our own anxiety so we can lead faithfully. Thanks for a great year and many more to come!"

**

There are no perfect congregations, just as there are no perfect people. Leadership in these times is as challenging as it has ever been. Our hope and prayer is that this book will help leaders remain clear, calm, and connected. This is the leader who will focus on self, not others; process, not content; strength, not weakness; challenge, not comfort; integrity, not unity; systems, not symptoms; and direction, not condition. May you be blessed in your journey and faithfully follow the one who brought all things into being, the one who redeems our brokenness, and the one who is present with us through everything this life brings.